Reading 4

A Revised Edition of
Global Views

• •

M. E. Sokolik

HEINLE & HEINLE
★
THOMSON LEARNING

United States • Australia • Canada • Mexico • Singapore • Spain • United Kingdom

For my brother and sister, Katherine & Charles, in no particular order

HEINLE & HEINLE

THOMSON LEARNING

Developmental Editors: Jennifer Monaghan, Jill Korey O'Sullivan
Sr. Production Coordinator: Maryellen E. Killeen
Market Development Director: Charlotte Sturdy
Sr. Manufacturing Coordinator: Mary Beth Hennebury
Interior Design: Julia Gecha
Illustrations: Pre-Press Company, Inc., Len Shalansky, Antonio Castro

Photo Research: Martha Friedman
Cover Design: Ha Nguyen Design
Cover Images: PhotoDisc®
Composition/Production: Pre-Press Company, Inc.
Freelance Production Editor: Janet McCartney
Copyeditor: Timothy Lemire
Printer/Binder: Bawden

For permission to use material from this text, contact us:

web	www.thomsonrights.com
fax	1-800-730-2215
phone	1-800-730-2214

For photo credits, see page 222.

Heinle & Heinle Publishers
20 Park Plaza
Boston, MA 02116

UK/EUROPE/MIDDLE EAST:
Thomson Learning
Berkshire House
168-173 High Holborn
London, WC1V 7AA, United Kingdom

AUSTRALIA/NEW ZEALAND:
Nelson/Thomson Learning
102 Dodds Street
South Melbourne
Victoria 3205 Australia

CANADA:
Nelson/Thomson Learning
1120 Birchmount Road
Scarborough, Ontario
Canada M1K 5G4

LATIN AMERICA:
Thomson Learning
Seneca, 53
Colonia Polanco
11560 México D.F. México

ASIA (excluding Japan):
Thomson Learning
60 Albert Street #15-01
Albert Complex
Singapore 189969

JAPAN:
Thomson Learning
Palaceside Building, 5F
1-1-1 Hitotsubashi, Chiyoda-ku
Tokyo 100 0003, Japan

SPAIN:
Thomson Learning
Calle Magallanes, 25
28015-Madrid
España

Library of Congress Cataloging-in-Publication Data
Sokolik, M. E. (Margaret E.)
   Tapestry reading 4 / M. E. Sokolik.
      p. cm.
   ISBN 0-8384-0060-4 (acid-free paper)
   1. English language—Textbooks for foreign speakers. 2. Readers. I. Title: Tapestry reading four. II. Title.

PE1128 .S5945 2000
428.6'4—dc21   99-054092

 This book is printed on acid-free recycled paper.

Printed in the United States of America.
2 3 4 5 6 7 8 9 03 02 01 00

A VERY SPECIAL THANK YOU

The publisher and authors would like to thank the following coordinators and instructors who have offered many helpful insights and suggestions for change throughout the development of the new *Tapestry*.

Alicia Aguirre, *Cañada College*
Fred Allen, *Mission College*
Maya Alvarez-Galvan, *University of Southern California*
Geraldine Arbach, *Collège de l'Outaouais, Canada*
Dolores Avila, *Pasadena City College*
Sarah Bain, *Eastern Washington University*
Kate Baldus, *San Francisco State University*
Fe Baran, *Chabot College*
Gail Barta, *West Valley College*
Karen Bauman, *Biola University*
Liza Becker, *Mt. San Antonio College*
Leslie Biaggi, *Miami-Dade Community College*
Andrzej Bojarczak, *Pasadena City College*
Nancy Boyer, *Golden West College*
Glenda Bro, *Mt. San Antonio College*
Brooke Brummitt, *Palomar College*
Linda Caputo, *California State University, Fresno*
Alyce Campbell, *Mt. San Antonio College*
Barbara Campbell, *State University of New York, Buffalo*
Robin Carlson, *Cañada College*
Ellen Clegg, *Chapman College*
Karin Cintron, *Aspect ILS*
Diane Colvin, *Orange Coast College*
Martha Compton, *University of California, Irvine*
Nora Dawkins, *Miami-Dade Community College*
Beth Erickson, *University of California, Davis*
Charles Estus, *Eastern Michigan University*
Gail Feinstein Forman, *San Diego City College*
Jeffra Flaitz, *University of South Florida*
Kathleen Flynn, *Glendale Community College*
Ann Fontanella, *City College of San Francisco*
Sally Gearhart, *Santa Rosa Junior College*
Alice Gosak, *San José City College*
Kristina Grey, *Northern Virginia Community College*
Tammy Guy, *University of Washington*
Gail Hamilton, *Hunter College*
Patty Heiser, *University of Washington*
Virginia Heringer, *Pasadena City College*

Catherine Hirsch, *Mt. San Antonio College*
Helen Huntley, *West Virginia University*
Nina Ito, *California State University, Long Beach*
Patricia Jody, *University of South Florida*
Diana Jones, *Angloamericano, Mexico*
Loretta Joseph, *Irvine Valley College*
Christine Kawamura, *California State University, Long Beach*
Gregory Keech, *City College of San Francisco*
Kathleen Keesler, *Orange Coast College*
Daryl Kinney, *Los Angeles City College*
Maria Lerma, *Orange Coast College*
Mary March, *San José State University*
Heather McIntosh, *University of British Columbia, Canada*
Myra Medina, *Miami-Dade Community College*
Elizabeth Mejia, *Washington State University*
Cristi Mitchell, *Miami-Dade Community College*
Sylvette Morin, *Orange Coast College*
Blanca Moss, *El Paso Community College*
Karen O'Neill, *San José State University*
Bjarne Nielsen, *Central Piedmont Community College*
Katy Ordon, *Mission College*
Luis Quesada, *Miami-Dade Community College*
Gustavo Ramírez Toledo, *Colegio Cristóbol Colón, Mexico*
Nuha Salibi, *Orange Coast College*
Alice Savage, *North Harris College*
Dawn Schmid, *California State University, San Marcos*
Mary Kay Seales, *University of Washington*
Denise Selleck, *City College of San Francisco*
Gail Slater, *Brooklyn and Staten Island Superintendency*
Susanne Spangler, *East Los Angeles College*
Karen Stanley, *Central Piedmont Community College*
Sara Storm, *Orange Coast College*
Margaret Teske, *ELS Language Centers*
Maria Vargas-O'Neel, *Miami-Dade Community College*
James Wilson, *Mt. San Antonio College and Pasadena City College*
Karen Yoshihara, *Foothill College*

ACKNOWLEDGMENTS

Thanks to Erik Rogers for his assistance in developing the instructor's manual and for his insightful comments on the discussion questions. Thanks also to Jill Kinkade for her help with the CNN video. I would especially like to thank Erik Gundersen for his capable and thoughtful guidance throughout the development of this series. Finally, and most importantly, love and thanks to Jim Duber for his support and help throughout this writing/editing process.

Tapestry Reading 4: Contents

ACADEMIC POWER STRATEGIES	CNN VIDEO CLIPS	READING OPPORTUNITIES
Get organized in order to do well in your studies.	"Hong Kong's Return to China" A discussion of the transfer of Hong Kong from British rule back to Chinese rule in 1997.	Reading 1: an essay about recent changes in Europe, the former Soviet Union, and the Czech Republic Reading 2: a magazine article about post-apartheid South Africa Reading 3: two essays representing different points of view about the return of Hong Kong to China
Organize a study group to learn more from your assignments.	"The Sierra Club Controversy" A look at the controversial debate within the Sierra Club about immigration control.	Reading 1: statistics about the world's population Reading 2: a poem Reading 3: a newspaper article about immigration and population growth Reading 4: a fictional story about adjusting to a new culture and prejudices
Expand your reading experience to become a better reader.	"Ragin' Cajuns" The culture and language of the Cajuns are being maintained in Louisiana. This report examines how.	Reading 1: a newspaper article about the debate over making English the official language of the United States Reading 2: a definition of the role of language Reading 3: an article about how babies learn language Reading 4: a newspaper article about language use in Canada
Manage your time to finish your assignments more efficiently.	"Istanbul Dining" A look at the foods and dining style native to the Turkish culture.	Reading 1: a quiz to determine your typical eating patterns and food decisions Reading 2: a research article about the diet in America Reading 3: an article examining the eating habits in different cultures
Read newspapers and magazines to stay informed about current issues and arguments.	"Child Labor" A discussion of the problem of child labor and the steps being taken to keep companies from hiring workers illegally.	Reading 1: an essay about child labor in India Reading 2: an essay about child labor in the United States Reading 3: a persuasive essay about a company's labor problems

ACADEMIC POWER STRATEGIES	CNN VIDEO CLIPS	READING OPPORTUNITIES
Learn to contribute to class discussion with more confidence to feel more comfortable in all of your classes.	"King Hussein of Jordan" Coverage of the funeral of this leader gives viewers a look at the king's life and accomplishments.	Reading 1: an essay by a person who was in the military and at Pearl Harbor during World War II Reading 2: an essay by a person who was in the military and at Hiroshima during World War II Reading 3: an article explaining an innovative approach to solving conflicts in the Middle East Reading 4: a poem
Find service learning opportunities in order to help your community while expanding your skills.	"Medicine Hunters" The importance of rain forests as potential resources for new drugs and the forces that threaten their existence.	Reading 1: an article about the benefits tropical rain forests can offer and the threats they face Reading 2: a magazine story about the damage humans are doing to the oceans Reading 3: a report on global warming Reading 4: a poem
Interview people in your community to expand your learning.	"Exotic Travel" Exotic vacation destinations and the people visiting them.	Reading 1: an article about the effects of tourism in Jamaica Reading 2: an excerpt from an essay on the positive side of travel and being a tourist Reading 3: an excerpt from an essay on the negative side of travel and being a tourist Reading 4: a chapter from an adventure travel book
Find ways to overcome procrastination so that you will get more work done.	"The Beijing Bicycle Ban" The once bicycle-friendly city imposes a ban on bicycles on its crowded streets.	Reading 1: a newspaper article about the battle between bicycles and cars in Beijing Reading 2: a radio report about a program to provide free bicycles for public use in San Francisco Reading 3: an article about an alternative type of car Reading 4: a magazine article about vehicles of the future
Accept your mistakes as part of the learning process.	"Multi-Media Education" An explanation of multi-media education and the advantages of this kind of learning.	Reading 1: an article about the international effects of the Internet Reading 2: an essay about media literacy, or an understanding of how television stories and programming can manipulate viewers Reading 3: a newspaper article about National TV-Turnoff Week, when people turn off their televisions for one week Reading 4: a report about the merging of the Internet and television

Welcome to TAPESTRY!

Empower your students with the **Tapestry Reading** series!

Language learning can be seen as an ever-developing tapestry woven with many threads and colors. The elements of the tapestry are related to different language skills such as listening and speaking, reading, and writing; the characteristics of the teachers; the desires, needs, and backgrounds of the students; and the general second language development process. When all of these elements are working together harmoniously, the result is a colorful, continuously growing tapestry of language competence of which the student and the teacher can be proud.

Tapestry is built upon a framework of concepts that helps students become proficient in English and prepared for the academic and social challenges in college and beyond. The following principles underlie the instruction provided in all of the components of the **Tapestry** program:

- Empowering students to be responsible for their learning
- Using Language Learning Strategies and Academic Power Strategies to enhance one's learning, both in and out of the classroom
- Offering motivating activities that recognize a variety of learning styles
- Providing authentic and meaningful input to heighten learning and communication
- Learning to understand and value different cultures
- Integrating language skills to increase communicative competence
- Providing goals and ongoing self-assessment to monitor progress

Guide to **Tapestry Reading**

Setting Goals focuses students' attention on the learning they will do in each chapter.

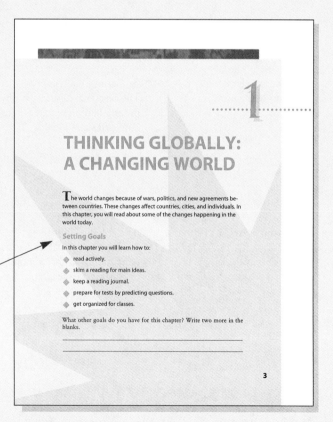

1

THINKING GLOBALLY: A CHANGING WORLD

The world changes because of wars, politics, and new agreements between countries. These changes affect countries, cities, and individuals. In this chapter, you will read about some of the changes happening in the world today.

Setting Goals

In this chapter you will learn how to:

- read actively.
- skim a reading for main ideas.
- keep a reading journal.
- prepare for tests by predicting questions.
- get organized for classes.

What other goals do you have for this chapter? Write two more in the blanks.

3

Stimulating reading selections from articles, stories, poems, interviews, essays, book excerpts, and more prepare students to read and comprehend a variety of academic texts.

Language Learning Strategies help students maximize their learning and become proficient in English.

Apply the Strategy activities encourage students to take charge of their learning and immediately use their new skills and strategies.

_____ amnesty   _____ confession   _____ suffocation
_____ apartheid   _____ reconciliation _____ testimony
_____ brink   _____ revenge

◆ **Read**

Reading 2: The Search For Truth in South Africa

"Only the truth can put the past to rest."
—*South African President Nelson Mandela*

1   Jeffrey Benzien, a police captain in South Africa, stood before a crowd of his fellow citizens and motioned with his hands. He was demonstrating a method of torture that would take victims to the **brink of suffocation**. Benzien admitted that he used this torture on people arrested for opposing the government. According to **testimony** reported last summer by the South African Press Association, Benzien said he tortured people "to protect the government."

2   Among the people who gathered to hear Benzien's **confession** last summer were several of his victims, including Tony Yengeni. It was Yengeni who had asked Benzien to demonstrate the torture method. "I wanted to see it with my own eyes—what he did to me," Yengeni said. "What kind of human being could do that?"

A History Of Injustice

3   Benzien's tale is just one of thousands of stories of violence and abuse told during the past two years in South Africa. Judges, ministers, and lawyers listen to these stories and record them as part of their work for the country's Truth and **Reconciliation** Commission. Their goal: to learn the facts about South Africa's troubled past.

4   Europeans first settled in what is now South Africa in the 1600s. These colonists set up a government and lived apart from native Africans. Even after South Africa became a self-ruling country in 1910, white people remained firmly in control.

5   From 1948 to 1994, the nation was ruled under a system known as **apartheid** (uh-par-tide). Apartheid kept blacks and whites apart: separate schools, separate neighborhoods, separate rights. No black person had the right to vote or take part in the government. In a nation of 32 million black people and 6 million whites, no black person had a voice.

6   Black South Africans and others who tried to fight this system were silenced quickly and sometimes violently. Thousands were thrown in prison. Hundreds were tortured and murdered by the police. White South African leaders looked away, even though these acts were against the law. They wanted white people to stay in power.

An End To White Rule

7   Apartheid could not last forever. After a long struggle, South Africa held its first open election in 1994. Once black citizens had a voice, they used it. They elected Nelson Mandela the country's first black president. He had spent 27 years in prison for fighting for black equality.

8   As white rule ca... feared that blacks w... cruelties of aparthe... ment and Mandela... deal. People who h... against apartheid c... protection from pu... thing: tell the truth...

◆ **After You Read**

Skimming: Getting the Main Ideas

After skimming the article, answer these questions:

1. What is the main idea of this reading?
2. What is the relationship of the United States and Europe, according to Mr. Havel?
3. What will happen if Europe becomes one, according to the reading?

Now read the article more closely. Remember to use the *active reading* strategies described at the beginning of the chapter.

LANGUAGE LEARNING STRATEGY

Keep a reading journal to help you keep track of your ideas and your learning. Keep your written responses to your readings together in a journal. This will help you to review your ideas, remember your reading, and more fully understand what you have read. You can keep your journal in a section of a notebook, a separate notebook, or on a computer disk. Use whatever is most convenient for you.

Apply the Strategy

Review your notes from the reading. What questions did you have? What ideas did you agree with or disagree with? Write a paragraph responding to the reading in your journal. In your response, you should discuss your own ideas and questions about the reading. Don't summarize it, but talk about your own reaction to it. You can also include questions about things you didn't understand.

Understanding and Communicating Ideas

A. Underline two passages in the reading that you found difficult to understand. Discuss those passages with a partner, and look up words you don't know. Then, rewrite those passages, putting them into your own words.

1. Paragraph number _____ New version: _____

   _____

   _____

Tapestry Threads provide students with interesting facts and quotes that jumpstart classroom discussions.

CNN® video clips provide authentic input and expand the readings to further develop language skills.

Academic Power Strategies give students the knowledge and skills to become successful, independent learners.

Getting Started

What is food to one man may be fierce poison to others.

—LUCRETIUS (95–55 B.C.E.),
DE RARUM NATURA

This chapter looks at food and dietary habits. Read these titles:

- "Do You Eat Smart?" a quiz from the *Los Angeles Times*
- "America Weighs In," a research article by Shannon Dortch
- "A Pyramid of Health," an article by Daniel Rogov

1. Based on these titles, predict the ideas this chapter will cover. List them here. _____

2. What do you already know about healthy eating? _____

3. What kind of diet does your home country have? _____

4. Look ahead at the pictures and charts in this chapter. What do these tell you about the topic of the chapter? _____

5. What do you want to learn from this chapter? Write down two questions you have about food and diet. _____

TUNING IN: "Istanbul Dining"

© CNN

Watch the CNN video about Istanbul dining. Discuss these questions with your class:

- What kinds of food are served in Istanbul?
- Describe what mealtimes are like in Istanbul.
- How does the Turkish style of eating compare with the style of eating in your native culture?

ACADEMIC POWER STRATEGY

Read newspapers and magazines to stay informed about current issues and arguments. Many students find they don't have enough time to keep up with current events. They stop reading newspapers and magazines when they go to college because they have so much reading to do for their courses. However, reading about current events can help you in your course work.

- Many problems in courses such as history, sociology, or psychology, have direct connections to current events. Knowing what those events are will help you to put your course reading into context.
- Reading newspapers and magazines provides you with reading practice.
- Reading about current events helps you to understand how people assemble their arguments.

Apply the Strategy

Find a weekly news magazine and bring it to class. Read one of the main news articles in it. Complete the following information, and discuss the article with your class:

Title: _____

Magazine: _____

Brief Summary: _____

What controversies are there over this topic? _____

What groups of people are involved? _____

What connections do you see to any of your college courses? _____

Test-Taking Tips offer students practical steps for improving their test results.

Check Your Progress helps students monitor their own progress.

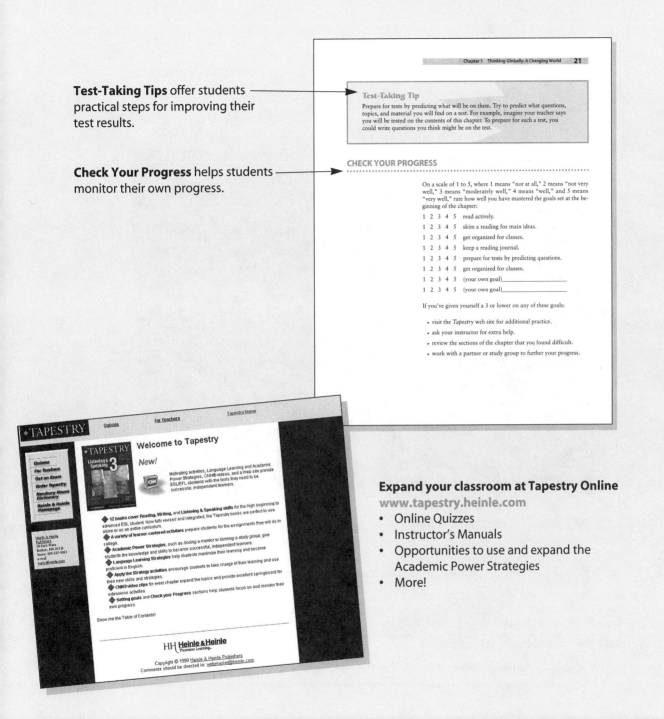

Test-Taking Tip

Prepare for tests by predicting what will be on them. Try to predict what questions, topics, and material you will find on a test. For example, imagine your teacher says you will be tested on the contents of this chapter. To prepare for such a test, you could write questions you think might be on the test.

CHECK YOUR PROGRESS

On a scale of 1 to 5, where 1 means "not at all," 2 means "not very well," 3 means "moderately well," 4 means "well," and 5 means "very well," rate how well you have mastered the goals set at the beginning of the chapter:

1 2 3 4 5   read actively.

1 2 3 4 5   skim a reading for main ideas.

1 2 3 4 5   get organized for classes.

1 2 3 4 5   keep a reading journal.

1 2 3 4 5   prepare for tests by predicting questions.

1 2 3 4 5   get organized for classes.

1 2 3 4 5   (your own goal)_____

1 2 3 4 5   (your own goal)_____

If you've given yourself a 3 or lower on any of these goals:

- visit the *Tapestry* web site for additional practice.
- ask your instructor for extra help.
- review the sections of the chapter that you found difficult.
- work with a partner or study group to further your progress.

Expand your classroom at Tapestry Online
www.tapestry.heinle.com
- Online Quizzes
- Instructor's Manuals
- Opportunities to use and expand the Academic Power Strategies
- More!

For a well-integrated curriculum, try the **Tapestry Writing** series and the **Tapestry Listening & Speaking** series, also from Heinle & Heinle.

To learn more about the **Tapestry** principles, read *The Tapestry of Language Learning*, Second Edition, by Rebecca L. Oxford and Robin C. Scarcella, also from Heinle & Heinle Publishers. ISBN 0-8384-2359-0.

Look at the photo. Then discuss these questions with your classmates:

- What is the setting of this photo?
- Who are these people?
- Would you like to visit or work there?

THINKING GLOBALLY: A CHANGING WORLD

The world changes because of wars, politics, and new agreements between countries. These changes affect countries, cities, and individuals. In this chapter, you will read about some of the changes happening in the world today.

Setting Goals

In this chapter you will learn how to:

- read actively.
- skim a reading for main ideas.
- keep a reading journal.
- prepare for tests by predicting questions.
- get organized for classes.

What other goals do you have for this chapter? Write two more in the blanks.

_____

_____

◆**Getting Started**

This chapter explores changes in three places: Europe, South Africa, and China. Look at these titles:

"The Chance that Will Not Return," an essay by Vaclav Havel, former president of the Czech Republic

"The Search for Truth in South Africa," a magazine article

"Hong Kong: Two Views," essays by Queen Elizabeth of England and Brian Becker

1. Predict the ideas that this chapter will cover. List them here.

_____

_____

_____

_____

2. What do you already know about South Africa's history?

_____

_____

_____

_____

3. What do you already know about Hong Kong and China?

_____

_____

_____

_____

4. What do you already know about recent changes in Europe?

_____

_____

_____

_____

5. Look ahead at the pictures and charts in this chapter. What do these tell you about the topic of the chapter?

_____

_____

_____

_____

6. What do you want to learn from this chapter? Write down two questions you have about the changing world.

_____

_____

_____

LANGUAGE LEARNING STRATEGY

Read actively to help you enjoy, understand, and better remember what you read. Active reading means reading critically, or questioning, what you read. When you read actively, you have a "conversation" with the author of the text, asking questions and arguing with ideas you don't agree with. This process not only helps you understand the reading better, but also makes reading a more enjoyable activity.

Active reading involves these five steps:

1. _Preparing to Read:_ When you prepare to read, look over the entire reading passage. Look at the photos, illustrations, titles, headings, and anything else that can give you an idea of what the reading is about. Then think about what you _already_ know about the subject. Note any vocabulary that looks unfamiliar, and look it up in your dictionary.

2. _Reading/Thinking:_ Read the text actively. Connect the ideas you read about to things you already know. Consider any new ideas, and think about how to combine them with ideas you already have.

3. _Marking and Questioning:_ Use a pencil to mark your book.[1] Here are some guidelines:

   • Underline important sentences, such as definitions or main ideas.

   • Mark important vocabulary items.

(continued on next page)

[1]If you aren't allowed to write in your book, use "sticky notes." You can write your notes on these pieces of paper, then stick them temporarily to the pages of your book.

- Summarize the topic of the paragraph in the margin.

- Write questions in the margin when you don't understand something.

- Make notes to remind yourself of questions or comments to bring to class.

- Indicate ideas with which you disagree.

4. *Reviewing:* After you have carefully read and marked your text, review the notes you have made. Reread any passages that you had difficulty understanding.

5. *Responding:* Write about or discuss the reading. This will help you remember your reading better, and be able to discuss it with confidence, whether informally, on a test, or in an essay.

Apply the Strategy

As you use this book, you will find many opportunities to use these techniques in your reading. Use the five steps above to read and respond to the first reading.

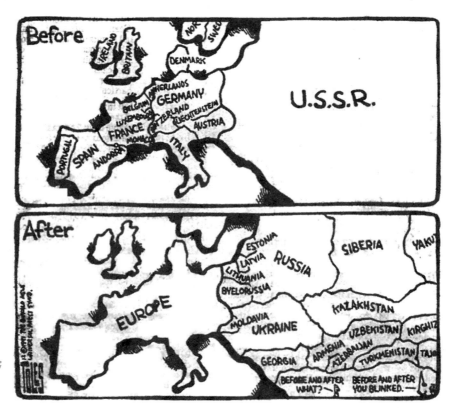

Drawing by Toles;
© 1991 Universal
Press Syndicate.

◇ Getting Ready to Read

Think About the Issues

Look at the cartoon on page 6. With a partner, discuss the meaning of this cartoon. Its meaning is related to the reading in this chapter. Make some notes about your discussion here:

_____

_____

_____

_____

_____

_____

Vocabulary Check

These words are found in the reading. Check those that you know. Discuss the words with a classmate, and explain any that you know but your partner does not. Use a dictionary, if necessary. Then, write a definition or example sentence in a vocabulary log. A vocabulary log is a notebook or section of a notebook used to record new words and phrases.

_____ gravitate

_____ ideology

_____ incarnation

_____ totalitarian

_____ undermine

Reading Focus: Skimming

Skimming a reading passage will help you to understand the main idea. Skimming means reading something quickly to get the main idea. When you skim you should:

- read the title and subheadings carefully.
- keep your eyes moving quickly over the text.
- look for "key" words that will give you important information about the text.

Skim the following reading. For your first reading, take only *one minute*. Then answer the questions that follow it.

Read

In 1993 Czechoslovakia became two independent countries: the Czech Republic and Slovakia.

Reading 1: The Chance that Will Not Return

by Vaclav Havel[1]

1 What kind of place could or should the new Europe be? What principles would hold this community together and what could it contribute to the rest of the world?

2   The spirit of history moves in mysterious ways, and it is hardly possible to pose a definite answer to these questions. But perhaps it is possible to glimpse in the mist of the unknown an outline of the place that Europe could become.

3   First of all, because Europe is as much an idea as a place, it would have to remain bigger than a sum of its parts. Any concept of a new Europe will have to deal with the existence of the United States and the Soviet Union[2], and not only for political reasons.

4   The United States, though completely outside Europe, is not entirely non-European. It was born out of Europe in a rebellion against it. The Soviet Union, though not completely inside Europe, has **gravitated** toward Europe for centuries, without ever taking the final step. In this century, the U.S. and the Soviet Union fought a war against a **totalitarian ideology** that threatened to **undermine** the very idea of Europe. Then, they almost fought each other over another **incarnation** of totalitarianism. If that had happened, the battlefield almost certainly would have been Europe once again. Thus both the Americans and the Russians, though in different degrees, may lay claims on the loyalty of Europeans. And both, fighting as they have for control of the continent, have earned different measures of distrust from Europeans.

5   If Europe becomes whole, it will have no need for guardians or protectors. But there should always be a place in Europe for the United States, the strongest democracy in the world. And there should be a place in Europe for a truly democratic Soviet Union. The histories and destinies of Europeans, Russians, and Americans are interlinked in countless ways.

[1]Vaclav Havel is a writer who became the leader of the Czech Republic after the "Velvet Revolution." During this Revolution, Czechoslovakia left Soviet rule, and split into two countries: the Czech Republic and Slovakia. The change in governments was peaceful and smooth (like "velvet").

[2]This article was written before the breakup of the Soviet Union. The Soviet Union is now Russia, Ukraine, Georgia, and a number of other independent countries.

After You Read

Skimming: Getting the Main Ideas

After skimming the article, answer these questions:

1. What is the main idea of this reading?

2. What is the relationship of the United States and Europe, according to Mr. Havel?

3. What will happen if Europe becomes one, according to the reading?

Now read the article more closely. Remember to use the *active reading* strategies described at the beginning of the chapter.

LANGUAGE LEARNING STRATEGY

Keep a reading journal to help you keep track of your ideas and your learning. Keep your written responses to your readings together in a journal. This will help you to review your ideas, remember your reading, and more fully understand what you have read. You can keep your journal in a section of a notebook, a separate notebook, or on a computer disk. Use whatever is most convenient for you.

Apply the Strategy

Review your notes from the reading. What questions did you have? What ideas did you agree with or disagree with? Write a paragraph responding to the reading in your journal. In your response, you should discuss your own ideas and questions about the reading. Don't summarize it, but talk about your own reaction to it. You can also include questions about things you didn't understand.

Understanding and Communicating Ideas

A. Underline two passages in the reading that you found difficult to understand. Discuss those passages with a partner, and look up words you don't know. Then, rewrite those passages, putting them into your own words.

1. Paragraph number _____ New version: _____

_____

_____

2. Paragraph number _____ New version: _____

_____

_____

B. These phrases are from the reading. Look at the reading again to see what they mean. Rewrite the sentences in your own words.

1. The spirit of history moves in mysterious ways.

_____

2. It is possible to glimpse in the mist of the unknown an outline of the place that Europe could become.

_____

3. It was born out of Europe in a rebellion against it.

_____

4. The Soviet Union has gravitated toward Europe.

_____

5. The histories and destinies of Europeans, Russians, and Americans are interlinked in countless ways.

_____

◆ **Getting Ready to Read**

The next reading deals with South Africa. Before you read, write in your *reading journal* everything you already know about South Africa. This will help you connect what you already know with the reading material. Also remember to mark this text so that you can respond to and review it.

Vocabulary Check

These words are found in the reading. Check those that you know. Discuss the words with a classmate, and explain any that you know but your partner does not. Use a dictionary, if necessary. Then, write a definition or example sentence in your Vocabulary Log.

———— amnesty   ———— confession   ———— suffocation

———— apartheid   ———— reconciliation   ———— testimony

———— brink   ———— revenge

◆**Read**   **Reading 2: The Search For Truth in South Africa**

"Only the truth can put the past to rest."
—South African President Nelson Mandela

1   Jeffrey Benzien, a police captain in South Africa, stood before a crowd of his fellow citizens and motioned with his hands. He was demonstrating a method of torture that would take victims to the **brink** of **suffocation**. Benzien admitted that he used this torture on people arrested for opposing the government. According to **testimony** reported last summer by the South African Press Association, Benzien said he tortured people "to protect the government."

2   Among the people who gathered to hear Benzien's **confession** last summer were several of his victims, including Tony Yengeni. It was Yengeni who had asked Benzien to demonstrate the torture method. "I wanted to see it with my own eyes—what he did to me," Yengeni said. "What kind of human being could do that?"

A History Of Injustice

3   Benzien's tale is just one of thousands of stories of violence and abuse told during the past two years in South Africa. Judges, ministers, and lawyers listen to these stories and record them as part of their work for the country's Truth and **Reconciliation** Commission. Their goal: to learn the facts about South Africa's troubled past.

4   Europeans first settled in what is now South Africa in the 1600s. These colonists set up a government and lived apart from native Africans. Even after South Africa became a self-ruling country in 1910, white people remained firmly in control.

5   From 1948 to 1994, the nation was ruled under a system known as **apartheid** (uh-par-tide). Apartheid kept blacks and whites apart: separate schools, separate neighborhoods, separate rights. No black person had the right to vote or take part in the government. In a nation of 32 million black people and 6 million whites, no black person had a voice.

6   Black South Africans and others who tried to fight this system were silenced quickly and sometimes violently. Thousands were thrown in prison. Hundreds were tortured and murdered by the police. White South African leaders looked away, even though these acts were against the law. They wanted white people to stay in power.

An End To White Rule

7   Apartheid could not last forever. After a long struggle, South Africa held its first open election in 1994. Once black citizens had a voice, they used it. They elected Nelson Mandela the country's first black president. He had spent 27 years in prison for fighting for black equality.

8   As white rule came to an end, many whites feared that blacks would seek **revenge** for the cruelties of apartheid. So the white government and Mandela's new government made a deal. People who had committed crimes for or against apartheid could receive **amnesty**—or protection from punishment—if they did one thing: tell the truth about their crimes.

The Healing Power Of Truth

9 Mandela and others felt that for South Africa's newborn democracy to grow strong, its people needed to face their ugly past. "We as a nation must confront the truth and heal ourselves," Mandela said.

10 And so the Truth and Reconciliation Commission began. People, white or black, who had committed crimes related to the struggle over apartheid were asked to come forward and admit to them. Others were ordered to appear before the commission. If a person confessed, he faced no punishment. Captain Benzien may have spoken up about his crimes because he knew he would not get in trouble.

11 Since the commission's first hearing in April 1996, more than 7,000 people have volunteered to tell the truth about past crimes. The commission members listen to testimony from white people who committed crimes to preserve apartheid and from black people who committed crimes while fighting apartheid. The commission meets in town halls and churches. Some hearings are even broadcast on television. By searching for the truth in such an open way, the commission hopes to help bring the people of South Africa together.

12 Not everyone supports the commission. Some victims' families want the people who hurt their loved ones to be punished. Others want to forget the past. One of them, P.W. Botha, was South Africa's president during some of the country's most violent times, from 1978 to 1989. He faces jail—not for any apartheid-era crimes he may have committed, but for refusing to appear before the commission. His trial is set for April.[1]

13 For now, the Truth Commission's sad work continues. Some stories the commission hears are so awful that the people listening can do nothing but cry. Parents learn the truth about how their children were murdered. Victims relive brutal beatings. The Truth Commission's chairman, Archbishop Desmond Tutu, has set up a special "crying room" outside some hearings. There, in that room, the tears of the people begin to wash clean the cuts of South Africa's past. There, in that room, a hurt nation begins to heal.

◆ After You Read

On September 23, 1998, President Clinton awarded the U.S. Congressional Gold Medal to South African President Nelson Mandela.

Comprehension

Discuss these questions, or write answers to them.

1. Who is Jeffrey Benzien?
2. What is the Truth and Reconciliation Commission?
3. When did South Africa achieve self-rule?
4. What was apartheid?
5. What happened to black South Africans who tried to protest the apartheid system?
6. Who was South Africa's first black president?

[1] As of June 1, 1999, Botha has refused to appear before the Truth and Reconciliation Commission. He was convicted of contempt of court, but that ruling was overturned.

7. How did some people get amnesty in South Africa?

8. Why was the amnesty program begun?

9. Who is P.W. Botha? Why is he facing jail time?

10. What is the "crying room"?

Analysis

In your *reading journal*, write your reaction to "The Search For Truth in South Africa." In particular, talk about the idea that the truth can help heal a nation. Do you agree with this idea? Why or why not?

◆ Vocabulary Building

Review the vocabulary from the beginning of the chapter. Discuss the words you don't know, or look them up in a dictionary. Then, show that you understand the words in bold letters by completing the sentence.

1. I am on the **brink** of _____.

2. **Suffocation** means you can't _____.

3. If you make a **confession,** you _____.

4. You often give **testimony** in _____.

5. If you have a **reconciliation,** you _____.

6. **Apartheid** was _____.

7. If you take **revenge,** you _____.

8. You might receive **amnesty** if _____.

◆ Getting Ready to Read

TUNING IN:
"Hong Kong's Return to China"

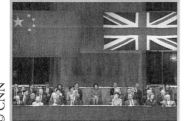
© CNN

Watch the CNN video about the transfer of Hong Kong back to China. Discuss these questions with your class:

- How long was Hong Kong under British rule?

- According to the polls, how do Hong Kong people feel about the return of Hong Kong to Chinese rule?

- What promises did the Chinese president make to Hong Kong?

- Why are pro-democracy and pro-union advocates worried?

- Why do experts say it's in Beijing's best interest to keep capitalism going in Hong Kong?

ACADEMIC POWER STRATEGY

Apply the Strategy

Get organized in order to do well in your studies. As a student, you need to keep track of lots of different kinds of information and assignments. Getting these things organized can really help you to become a better student.

Which of these things do you regularly do? Check them off the list. From the ones you don't regularly do, pick some new ones that you think will help you become more organized.

_____ keep a calendar of all my assignments and tests (see page 71 for more information on keeping a calendar)

_____ put all of my textbooks in one place so I can find them easily

_____ maintain notebooks or file folders for each of my classes to keep my notes in order

_____ keep my desktop neat so I can find things I need

_____ make "to do" lists to remind myself of important assignments

_____ make a place for important papers and records

_____ keep the files on my computer organized

Vocabulary Check

Which of these words do you already know? Check them off. Discuss the words with a classmate, and explain any that you know but your partner does not. Use a dictionary, if necessary. Then, write a definition or example sentence in your Vocabulary Log.

_____ bourgeoisie	_____ destitute	_____ garland (verb)
_____ convoy	_____ enclave	_____ hype
_____ cymbal	_____ exuberant	_____ imperialism

—— liaison   —— sovereignty

—— prodigiously   —— stipulate

The Opium Wars (1839–1843, 1856–1860) between Britain and China led to Britain's takeover of Hong Kong and part of the Kowloon Peninsula.

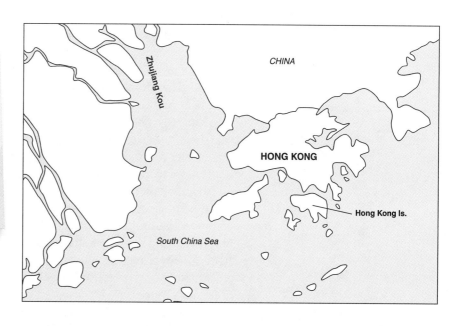

Read

The next readings represent two points of view about the return of Hong Kong to China. The first is written by the Queen of England, the second by a writer for an American Communist Party newspaper.

While you read these two articles, use the *active reading* techniques described earlier in this chapter. Be sure that you mark your text.

Reading 3: Hong Kong: Two Views

Britain and Hong Kong: A Part of Each Other's Future

Message from Her Majesty The Queen delivered by HRH[1] The Prince of Wales[2] at the British Farewell Ceremony, Hong Kong, 30 June 1997

1   Five hours from now, the Union Flag[3] will be lowered and the flag of China will fly over Hong Kong. More than a century and a half of British administration will come to an end.

2   During that time, Hong Kong has grown from a small coastal settlement into one of the leading cities and one of the greatest

[1]HRH means "His Royal Highness," which refers to his being a prince.

[2]This is a reference to Prince Charles, the former husband of Princess Diana.

[3]The flag of England

trading economies in the world. There have been times of sacrifice, suffering, and courage. As Hong Kong has risen from the ashes of war a most dramatic transformation has taken place. Millions of **destitute** immigrants have been absorbed and Hong Kong has created one of the most successful societies on earth.

3   Britain is both proud and privileged to have been involved with this success story. Proud of the British values and institutions that have been the framework for Hong Kong's success. Proud of the rights and freedoms which Hong Kong people enjoy. Privileged to have been associated with the **prodigiously** talented and resourceful people of Hong Kong who have built upon that foundation.

4   The British flag will be lowered and British administrative responsibility will end. But Britain is not saying goodbye to Hong Kong. More than three and a half million Hong Kong residents are British nationals. Thousands of young Hong Kong men and women study in Britain every year. We share language and the English common law. And thousands of Britons, too, have made their homes in Hong Kong. The shared legacy of family and of friendship, trade and investment, culture and history runs strong and deep.

5   Britain is part of Hong Kong's history and Hong Kong is part of Britain's history. We are also part of each other's future. We are confident that the ties between us will not only endure but will continue to develop. In a shrinking world, Hong Kong's role as Europe's gateway to Asia and Britain's role as Asia's gateway to Europe will reinforce the bonds between our two societies.

6   For all these reasons, my government and I will continue to take the closest interest in Hong Kong and in its development. The British Consulate-General, which will be inaugurated in a few hours' time, will be our largest in the world. The Sino[4]-British Joint **Liaison** Group will continue for another two and a half years to discuss matters concerning the implementation of the Sino-British Joint Declaration. That Joint Declaration itself remains in force for fifty years. For many years to come, the Hong Kong connection will command our attention.

7   Hong Kong now faces its transition to Chinese **sovereignty** in excellent condition—prosperous, stable and dynamic. Unprecedented though this moment in history may be, we have the utmost confidence in the abilities and resilience of the Hong Kong people. Britain learnt[5] long ago that Hong Kong people know best what is good for Hong Kong. We have no doubt that Hong Kong people can run Hong Kong, as the Joint Declaration promises, and that faithful implementation of the Joint Declaration is the key to Hong Kong's continued success.

[4]Sino is a prefix used to indicate "Chinese."

[5]"Learnt" is British English. "Learned" is American English.

8   The eyes of the world are on Hong Kong today. I wish you all a successful transition and a prosperous and peaceful future.

With Brits Out, It's Hong Kong, People's Republic of China

by Brian Becker

1   Joyous celebrations erupted throughout China at midnight June 30 as 155 years of British colonial domination over Hong Kong came to an end.

2   Ripped away from mainland China in the Opium War of 1839-1842 and then leased to Britain for 99 years in an imposed treaty in 1898, Hong Kong reverted to Chinese sovereignty in a peaceful transfer negotiated by the British and Chinese governments.

3   The agreement was made in 1984 between British Prime Minister Margaret Thatcher and Deng Xiaoping, leader of the People's Republic of China. Its essence **stipulated** that the British would pull out of Hong Kong and that for at least 50 years China would not interfere with the capitalist system that British and world **imperialism** have maintained in this deep-water harbor **enclave** on China's southern coast.

4   Under the slogan "one country, two systems," the PRC recovers sovereignty over the territory. But the big **bourgeoisie** in Hong Kong is guaranteed the "right" to maintain private property and vast fortunes.

5   The properties foreign capitalist corporations now own will also continue to belong to their current owners.

6   It is noteworthy that Mao Zedong[6] and the other early leaders of the PRC did not favor forcibly seizing Hong Kong, even when that was clearly possible from a military viewpoint.

Chinese troops welcomed

1   After all the media **hype** here on possible "panic" in Hong Kong, here's what really happened when Chinese troops arrived, according to a July 1 Associated Press[7] report:

2   "The often **exuberant** welcome indicated that many in Hong Kong don't mind having the People's Liberation Army[8] in their midst.

3   "At points along the **convoys**' routes, crowds of cheering, **cymbal**-clanging, drum-beating people turned out to greet the Chinese troops.

[6]Leader of the Chinese Communist Party, 1949-1976

[7]The Associated Press is an organization that writes and reports news stories that are purchased by newspapers and other news organizations.

[8]The People's Liberation Army is the army of the People's Republic of China.

4   "In the seaside suburb of Stanley, once a British redoubt[9], about 300 people stood in heavy rain to await the Chinese convoy heading to Stanley Fort. . . . When the 20 vehicles drove slowly by, people broke through police lines to shake hands with the soldiers and give them bouquets.

5   "'Very exciting,' declared 16-year-old Penguin Wong. . . . 'We are so happy about Hong Kong's return to China.'

6   ". . . In the semi-rural New Territories, . . . people turned out to cheer and beat drums as the troops crossed the border. Beaming Chinese officers got out of their cars and were **garlanded** with flowers."

After You Read

Comprehension

Discuss these questions, or write answers to them.

1. How long did Britain rule Hong Kong?

2. Why is Britain proud of its role in Hong Kong's development, according to the Queen?

3. Why does the Queen believe that Hong Kong and Britain will maintain a strong relationship?

4. What is the Sino-British Joint Declaration?

5. Why was Hong Kong originally transferred to British power?

6. Who is reponsible for the agreement to transfer Hong Kong back to China?

7. What are the details of the agreement between China and Britain?

8. What does "one country, two systems" mean?

9. What was the media "hype" about the transfer of power, according to the second article?

10. According to Becker, how did the people in Hong Kong react to the arrival of the Chinese Army?

Analysis

1. Compare the two points of view here. Find passages or quotations in the articles that show these points of view. Work with a partner, if you wish.

[9]redoubt = fort or citadel

Topic	Queen of England	Brian Becker
view of the Opium War	not mentioned in the readings	
views of the people of Hong Kong		
Britain's role in Hong Kong		

2. What is your opinion? Write about that opinion in a response to the readings. Write it in your *reading journal.*

> ◄ **Vocabulary Building**

Each of the words in the table has a *synonym* somewhere in the list of vocabulary items before the reading. Find the word with a similar meaning in the reading and write it in the second column. The first one is done for you as an example.

1. authority   _____*sovereignty*_____

2. connection   _____

3. domination   _____

4. very poor   _____

5. propaganda   _____

6. wreath   _____

7. specify   _____

8. enthusiastic   _____

9. area within an area   _____

10. procession   _____

PUTTING IT ALL TOGETHER

In this chapter, you learned:

- to read actively.
- to skim a reading to get its main idea quickly.
- to keep a reading journal.

Practice these skills as you do the following activities.

Read More

Find an article in a newspaper, magazine, or on the Internet that talks about a change happening in the world today. Read the article, then write in your *reading journal* about it. Discuss some of these ideas:

- Ideas in the article that interested you
- Parts that you didn't understand
- How this story relates to your life, or to someone you know

Then, report to your class about the article you found.

Discuss

What is the most important change going on in the world right now, in your opinion? In a group of three or four people, discuss your ideas. Prepare for your discussion by completing the following notes:

1. The most important change happening in the world today is

   _____

   _____

2. The background of this change is _____

   _____

3. I think this change is important because _____

   _____

Express your opinion in your group. Listen to the others' ideas as well.

Write

Everyone is affected by changes in the world. Think about a global change that has affected your life in some way. It might be something that has *directly* affected you or your family or it might be an *indirect* change. Think about a change and write about it.

Test-Taking Tip

Prepare for tests by predicting what will be on them. Try to predict what questions, topics, and material you will find on a test. For example, imagine your teacher says you will be tested on the contents of this chapter. To prepare for such a test, you could write questions you think might be on the test.

CHECK YOUR PROGRESS

On a scale of 1 to 5, where 1 means "not at all," 2 means "not very well," 3 means "moderately well," 4 means "well," and 5 means "very well," rate how well you have mastered the goals set at the beginning of the chapter:

1 2 3 4 5   read actively.

1 2 3 4 5   skim a reading for main ideas.

1 2 3 4 5   get organized for classes.

1 2 3 4 5   keep a reading journal.

1 2 3 4 5   prepare for tests by predicting questions.

1 2 3 4 5   get organized for classes.

1 2 3 4 5   (your own goal)_____

1 2 3 4 5   (your own goal)_____

If you've given yourself a 3 or lower on any of these goals:

- visit the *Tapestry* web site for additional practice.

- ask your instructor for extra help.

- review the sections of the chapter that you found difficult.

- work with a partner or study group to further your progress.

L ook at the photo. Then discuss these questions with your classmates.

- What is happening in this photo?
- Have you or has someone you know been through this ceremony?
- Why is this ceremony held?

ON THE MOVE: POPULATION AND IMMIGRATION

In Chapter 1, you read about some of the recent changes in Europe, Asia, and Africa. People often immigrate because of political or economic changes in their native countries. In some cases, these changes cause some populations to move from one country to another. This chapter explores some reasons for and some effects of immigration.

Setting Goals

In this chapter you will learn how to:

- identify and understand different purposes for reading.

- organize a study group.

- summarize a reading's main points.

- recognize and understand compound words.

- ask questions to get information you need about tests.

What other goals do you have for this chapter? Write one or two of them here.

_____

_____

◆**Getting Started**

The writers in this chapter use different formats to tell their immigration stories: fiction, an essay, statistics, and a poem. While you read, think about which format you enjoy reading most, and why. Look at the titles of the readings for this chapter and answer the questions.

Readings

"Global Village," statistics about the world's population
"Lost Sister," a poem by Cathy Song
"Green Cards," a newspaper article by Patty Wentz
"Wilshire Bus," a fictional story by Hisaye Yamamoto

1. Predict the ideas that the readings will cover. List them here.

   _____

   _____

   _____

2. What are two things you already know about immigration to the U.S. and Canada?

   _____

   _____

   _____

3. Refer to the list of reading purposes on page 25. What do you think is the purpose of reading charts and graphs?

   _____

   _____

   _____

4. Look ahead at the photos and illustrations in this chapter. What do these tell you about the topic of the readings?

   _____

   _____

   _____

5. What do you want to learn from this chapter? Write down two questions you have about population and immigration.

   _____

   _____

   _____

LANGUAGE LEARNING STRATEGY

Identify and understand different purposes for reading assignments in order to complete them more efficiently. Just as there are many different types of reading, there are many purposes for reading. Often we read for information. Sometimes the information is presented from a certain point of view. In these cases, we read to understand the point of view and consider whether we agree with it. Sometimes we read just for the pleasure of reading.

Among your course assignments, you will find that there are different purposes for reading. Understanding these purposes will help you complete your assignments more effectively and get more out of your reading.

Look at the list of reading purposes below. Check any that you have used. Can you think of others? Add them to the list.

1. _____ to get information about specific questions

2. _____ to check the accuracy of information you have

3. _____ to get a general understanding of a topic

4. _____ to understand an author's point of view or argument

5. _____ to check predictions you have made about a topic

6. _____ to enjoy reading

7. _____

8. _____

Apply the Strategy

When you are given a reading assignment in other classes, use this list to identify the purpose of the assignment. If you aren't sure, ask your instructor. Look at a reading assignment from one of your other classes. Write the name of the class and assignment here.

_____

_____

Write down one or two possible purposes for doing this particular reading.

_____

_____

Getting Ready to Read

Reading Focus: Reading Charts and Graphs

Not all reading is in text form. Sometimes your reading assignments include charts, graphs, and other visual information. Certain information, especially numbers and statistics, can be much more easily understood in a visual format. When you read a chart or graph, look for titles, dates, and source information to help you understand what is being shown.

It can be confusing to read text that contains many numbers and figures. Organizing the information into a visual format such as a graph or a chart can make it easier to understand and remember. This is especially helpful with readings in a business, science, or mathematics course.

Reading for Information

The reading that follows focuses on statistics. As you read it, try to create a graph, picture, or map to help illustrate one of the main ideas. For example, you might create a pie chart of the population:

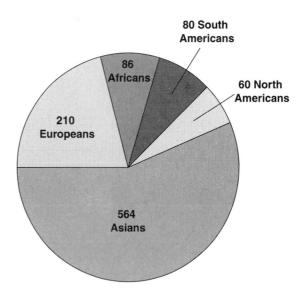

Read

Reading 1: The Global Village

If our world were a village of only 1,000 people, what would it look like? IRED Forum, a publication of *Innovations et Réseaux pour le Développement* ("Development Innovations and Networks") in Geneva, Switzerland, gives these approximate numbers:

In the village there would be:

564 Asians	80 South Americans
210 Europeans	60 North Americans
86 Africans	

There would be:

300 Christians (183 Catholics, 84 Protestants, 33 Orthodox)

175 Moslems	55 Buddhists
128 Hindus	1 Other
47 Animists[1]	

210 without any religion or atheist

Of these people:

60 would control half the total income	600 would live in shantytowns[2]
500 would be hungry	700 would be illiterate

After You Read

Analysis

Compare the graphic you created with a partner's. Discuss these questions:

1. What graphic did you create?

2. Why did you choose it?

3. How does it illustrate and clarify for you the ideas in the reading?

ACADEMIC POWER STRATEGY

Organize a study group to learn more from your assignments. The saying "two heads are better than one" definitely applies to studying. If you can find a group of classmates to study with, you will find the task more pleasant. You'll probably learn more, too.

(continued on next page)

[1]Animists are people who believe that natural elements, such as trees or rivers, have souls.

[2]Shantytowns are residential areas in which the extremely poor live. "Shanties" are poorly constructed huts, often made of tin or cardboard.

Apply the Strategy

Take these steps to organize a study group:

- Identify a group of classmates with whom you would like to study.
- Compare your schedules and set regular meeting times.
- Schedule a first meeting to set your goals.
- Make a telephone and e-mail list of all the members so you can contact each other easily.

After your study group meets, report on the meeting in class.

◆ Getting Ready to Read

Reading for Insight

This reading is a poem. Even though a poem can be a source of information, you read a poem differently than you read an article or a story. A poem can give you an understanding of another person or culture. You should read the poem more than once, and read it aloud to hear the sounds of the words. What is the purpose of reading a poem, in your opinion? Write a short entry in your journal in answer to this question.

On July 1, 1900 the U.S. population was near 76 million. On July 1, 1998 it was over 270 million.

Vocabulary Check

This poem may have many words that are new to you. Check the words that you already know. Because there are many words in this list, find a partner and compare your lists. If you know a word your partner doesn't know, explain it to him or her. Use a dictionary, if necessary. You can add new words you learn to your Vocabulary Log.

In 1882, the Chinese Exclusion Act was created to stop Chinese immigration to the U.S.

_____ arc	_____ jade	_____ spew
_____ dormant	_____ locusts	_____ strangulate
_____ ferment	_____ meager	_____ swarm
_____ flimsy	_____ provisions	_____ unremitting
_____ glisten	_____ redundant	_____ willow
_____ inundate	_____ relinquish	

Read

As you read the poem, think about the questions in the right column. Add questions of your own, then discuss them with your classmates after you have finished the poem.

Reading 2: Lost Sister

Who is the "lost sister"? Read the poem to find out.

by Cathy Song

1
In China, even the peasants named
their first daughters
jade—
the stone that in the far fields
could moisten the dry season,   *How could a stone "moisten" the dry season?*
could make men move mountains   *Why would men "move mountains"?*
for the healing green of the inner hills
glistening like slices of winter melon.   *Why does the poet compare jade to melons?*

And the daughters were grateful:
They never left home.   *Why did the daughters stay home?*
To move freely was a luxury
stolen from them at birth.
Instead, they gathered patience,
learning to walk in shoes   *Why did they walk in "shoes the size of teacups"?*
the size of teacups,
without breaking—
the **arc** of their movements
as **dormant** as the rooted **willow**,   *What does it mean to be "dormant"?*
as **redundant** as the farmyard hens.
But they traveled far   *What does it mean that the daughters "traveled far"?*
in surviving,
learning to stretch the family rice,
to quiet the demons,
the noisy stomachs.

2
There is a sister   *Who is the sister?*
across the ocean,
who **relinquished** her name,
diluting jade green   *How did she "dilute" jade?*
with the blue of the Pacific.
Rising with a tide of **locusts**,
she **swarmed** with others
to **inundate** another shore.   *Where is the sister?*
In America,
there are many roads   *What are the advantages of American life?*

and women can stride along with men.
But in another wilderness,
the possibilities,
the loneliness,
can **strangulate** like jungle vines.   *What are the problems listed here?*
The **meager provisions** and sentiments
of once belonging—   *What does the immigrant lose by being in a new*
fermented roots, Mah-Jong[1] tiles and   *country?*
firecrackers—set but
a **flimsy** household in a forest of nightless cities.
A giant snake rattles above,
spewing black clouds into your kitchen.
Dough-faced landlords   *What are "dough-faced" landlords?*
slip in and out of your keyholes,
making claims you don't understand,
tapping into your communication systems   *What does it mean to "tap into the communication*
of laundry lines and restaurant chains.   *systems"?*
You find you need China: *Why does she need China?*
your one fragile identification,
a jade link
handcuffed to your wrist.
You remember your mother
who walked for centuries,   *How could the mother walk for centuries?*
footless—
and like her,
you have left no footprints,   *Why has the narrator "left no footprints"?*
but only because
there is an ocean in between,
the **unremitting** space of your rebellion.   *What does this line mean?*

◆ After You Read

Analysis

A. Look at the questions in the right column. Add questions you have, if you haven't done so already. Then discuss these questions with your class.

1. Who is the narrator?

2. Who is the "lost sister"?

3. What is the main idea of the poem?

[1]Mah-Jong is a type of game played with tiles.

B. Imagery is writing that allows you to "see" what the writer is talking about. For example, "the stone that in the far fields could moisten the dry season" is an *image*. Locate five other images in the poem and write them here:

1. _____

2. _____

3. _____

4. _____

5. _____

Why do you think poets use imagery? How does it help you to understand the poem?

◆ Vocabulary Building

Compound Words

This poem contains several *compound words*, or words made up of two separate words. Each word below belongs to a compound word found in this poem. Working with a partner, and looking back at the poem, write a compound word to match each definition. The first one is done for you.

cracker	cuffs	~~cup~~
farm	fire	foot
hand	hole	key
land	lord	print
~~tea~~	yard	

1. You can drink out of it: _____ *teacup* _____

2. You celebrate the New Year with it: _____

3. You find cows and horses there: _____

4. He collects your rent each month: _____

5. Where a key is put to open a door: _____

6. They're used to restrain criminals: _____

7. You leave it in the sand: _____

TUNING IN:
"The Sierra Club Controversy"

© CNN

Watch the CNN video story about the Sierra Club. Discuss these questions with your class:

- What was the controversy in the Sierra Club?
- Why do some members support immigration control?
- Who founded the Sierra Club?
- Whose side do you find more convincing?

◆ Getting Ready to Read

Reading for Understanding

The next reading concerns immigration, population growth, and the Sierra Club. The author explains an argument within a group called the Sierra Club. Before you read, see if you can find the answers to these questions. Look on the Internet, or ask classmates or friends:

- Do you know what the world population is today?
- What are the effects of overpopulation?
- What is the Sierra Club?

Discuss with your class whether you think the world has an over-population problem.

Vocabulary Check

Which of these words do you already know? Check them. Work with a partner to find the meanings of new words. Use a dictionary, if necessary. You can add any new words you learn to your vocabulary log.

| _____ controversy | _____ infanticide | _____ legitimate |
| _____ divisive | _____ notorious | _____ woo |

◆ Read

The next reading is an article. It addresses a controversial subject: immigration as it affects population growth and the impact of both on the environment. The purpose of this reading is to understand different points of view about population, immigration, and the environment.

Reading 3: Green Cards

by Patty Wentz

1   Greg Jacob is a nice guy. He isn't considered mean-spirited, racist or foolish— even by fellow Sierra Club members. They say the Portland State University English professor is being fooled by people who only want to spread fear and racism.

2   "I think Greg is a very good-hearted person," says Ross Williams, a member of the Sierra Club. "He's always been fair to me. I don't think he quite understands what he's involved in."

3   Professor Jacob is involved in a **controversy** within the Sierra Club, the country's oldest and largest environmental group. Jacob, the chairman of the Oregon Sierra Club's population committee, has joined a small group of members around the country who say the Sierra Club should push to slow immigration into the United States.

4   The Sierra Club has long viewed population control as a means to reduce demands on natural resources. By opposing immigration, Jacob and other members in the traditionally liberal group have joined conservative anti-immigrant activists who want to close U.S. borders.

5   The immigration debate has been growing in the national Sierra Club for years. It will climax next week when ballots are mailed to the country's 550,000 members.[1] The members can vote to keep the current population policy, which is neutral on immigration, or adopt "Alternative A," which calls for an end to U.S. population growth, including a reduction in immigration.

6   Professor Jacob sees immigration as part of an overall population policy. This policy includes worldwide family planning and raising the standard of living for women. Americans are greedy and wasteful, he says, and as more people come here, they will adopt Americans' wasteful habits and continue to have children at the high birth rates of their own countries.

7   "Some people think it's **divisive** and racist to talk about net reduction in immigration," he says. "We are not racist. We are concerned about overpopulation, and that's an environmental issue."

8   Oregon has 12,220 Sierra Club members. While the immigration issue has caused a large debate, the state chapter has not taken an official position.

9   Williams opposes Alternative A and has led the debate within the Oregon Sierra Club. He says it harms efforts at global population control. "The Sierra Club is in the business of protecting the entire environment," he says, "not our own private environment."

10   Williams also says that while some members, such as Jacob, have **legitimate** concerns, he agrees that the debate is also supported by people whose biggest motivation is not conserving natural resources. "At one meeting, someone said to me, 'If you lived in Hillsboro [which has a large Latino population], you'd understand.'"

11   Williams says the anti-immigration forces have targeted the Sierra Club because of its democratic nature.

12   Rick Gwynallen of the Ashland, Oregon, environmental group Headwaters says the Sierra Club vote was a hot topic at a recent state conference. "There's a sense that it will be a big deal for environmental groups," he says. "If they ignore the issue, they run the risk of members being divided . . . they feel their memberships will be **wooed**." To prevent entering the debate, Headwaters recently became the first of these groups to issue a statement saying immigration is not an environmental concern.

13   The Federation for American Immigration Reform (FAIR), one of the most **notorious** immigrant-reform groups, strongly supports Kuper's initiative. The Weeden Foundation, one of the primary funders of FAIR, is financing a

[1]The Sierra Club voted to delay the decision.

mass mailing about the ballot to the national Sierra Club membership.

14   Other anti-immigration groups have encouraged people to join the Sierra Club in order to vote. Jacob says he's heard that pro-immigration forces have done the same. In any case, the Sierra Club, which had been losing members in recent years, has added more than 25,000 new members during the past few months.

15   What's disturbing to many environmentalists—particularly those who'd like to work more closely with minority communities— are signs of bigotry in the anti-immigration forces trying to influence the Sierra Club vote.

16   In a 1988 memo supporting immigration control (never intended to be made public), FAIR founder John Tanton wrote, "As whites see their power and control over their lives declining, will they simply go quietly into the night?" Garrett Hardin, a member of FAIR's board of directors, has been quoted as saying that sending food to Africa encourages people to overpopulate, and that **infanticide** is a valid population control method.

17   Jacob is surprised by such reports. Even though he quoted Hardin to *Willamette Week* newspaper, he says he was unaware of Hardin's extreme views. He believes many members of the Sierra Club support immigration limits for environmental reasons. He's angry about reports of outsiders joining the club in order to vote. He says, "I don't like the idea of people doing that. That goes against what I believe."

◆ After You Read

Comprehension

Discuss these questions with your class.

1. What is the Sierra Club?

2. Who is Professor Jacob? What is his opinion about immigation?

3. What is the debate about within the Sierra Club?

4. What is Alternative A?

5. Why do some people feel Alternative A is racist? Do you agree?

6. Why is population control an environmental issue, according to some members of the Sierra Club?

7. What is the double meaning of the title, "Green Cards"?

LANGUAGE LEARNING STRATEGY

Summarize main points in order to understand complex readings. In college-level texts, you often need to read complex passages that present a lot of information or more than one point of view. Summarizing helps you recognize what the most important points of the reading are and helps you better understand what you have read.

Apply the Strategy

The purpose of the previous article is to explain the issues and arguments about immigration reform and its impact on the environment. In response to the article, write a short summary of each side of the debate. Use the chart to help organize the information for your summary. One is done for you as an example.

For Immigration Reform	Against Immigration Reform
Who: *Greg Jacob* Reasons: *He believes the U.S. is in danger of becoming overpopulated.*	Who: Reasons:
Who: Reasons:	Who: Reasons:
Who: Reasons:	Who: Reasons:

In your journal, write your opinion. Which side do you support? Explain your reasons.

Reading Focus: Understanding Point of View

Roleplaying is a good way to explore the points of view in a reading. Review the reading. Form a group of three. Each person in your group should pick one of these roles:

- the Sierra Club president, who opposes Alternative A
- a Sierra Club member, who supports Alternative A
- a newspaper reporter, who wants to find out more about the issue

In your roleplay, be sure the first two characters explain their positions clearly. The newspaper reporter should prepare questions to ask before the roleplay.

◇Vocabulary Building

Match the words from the reading on the left with their meanings on the right. Look back at the reading for clues to the words' meanings.

_____ 1. controversy   a. dividing

_____ 2. divisive   b. disreputable

_____ 3. infanticide   c. debate

_____ 4. legitimate   d. killing of babies

_____ 5. notorious   e. charm

_____ 6. woo   f. rightful

Test-Taking Tip

Ask questions to get the information you need about a test. Make a list of all the things you need to know about your test—how long it is, whether you can use your notes or books, what material it covers, and so forth. If you are uncomfortable asking the questions in class, find out your instructor's office hours and ask privately. Or, ask before or after class. Be sure you have the answers to all your questions before the test.

◇ Getting Ready to Read

Reading for Enjoyment

The last reading in this chapter is a fictional story. The purpose of fiction is enjoyment, and also to learn about the author's ideas. Before you read, discuss these questions with a classmate:

- Do you enjoy reading short stories or novels?

- What kind of reading do you do in your leisure time?

- Has anyone ever made a racist comment to a friend or relative? How did you respond?

Vocabulary Check

Which of these words do you already know? Check them. Work with a partner to find the meanings of new words. Use a dictionary, if necessary. You can add any new words you learn to your Vocabulary Log.

_____ bespectacled	_____ emphatic	_____ pastoral
_____ chortle	_____ exclusion	_____ solicitous
_____ coolies	_____ gloating	_____ titter
_____ craw	_____ jovial	_____ unmitigated
_____ diatribe	_____ insidiously	_____ vicarious
_____ eloquence	_____ monologue	

After the bombing of Pearl Harbor, President Franklin D. Roosevelt ordered all persons of Japanese ancestry living on the West Coast to be held in internment camps. One hundred and twenty thousand people were taken to relocation centers and held there.

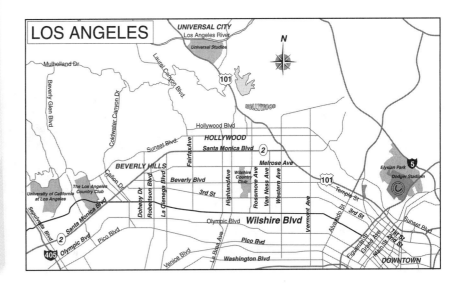

LOS ANGELES

Read

Reading 4: Wilshire Bus

by Hisaye Yamamoto

1   Wilshire Boulevard begins somewhere near the heart of downtown Los Angeles and, except for a few digressions scarcely worth mentioning, goes straight out to the edge of the Pacific Ocean. It is a wide boulevard and traffic on it is fairly fast. For the most part, it is bordered on either side with examples of the recent stark architecture which favors a great deal of glass. As the boulevard approaches the sea, however, the landscape becomes a bit more **pastoral**, so that the university and the soldiers' home there give the appearance of being huge country estates.

2   Esther Kuroiwa got to know this stretch of territory quite well while her husband Buro was in one of the hospitals at the soldiers' home. They had been married less than a year when his back, injured in the war, began troubling him again, and he was forced to take three months of treatments at Sawtelle before he was able to go back to work. During this time, Esther was permitted to visit him twice a week and she usually took the yellow bus out on Wednesdays because she did not know the first thing about driving and because her friends were not able to take her except on Sundays. She always enjoyed the long bus ride very much because her seat companions usually turned out to be amiable, and if they did not, she took **vicarious** pleasure in gazing out at the almost **unmitigated** elegance along the fabulous street.

3   It was on one of these Wednesday trips that Esther committed a grave sin of omission which caused her later to burst into tears and which caused her acute discomfort for a long time afterwards whenever something reminded her of it.

4   The man came on the bus quite early and Esther noticed him briefly as he entered because he said gaily to the driver, "You robber. All you guys do is take money from me every day, just for giving me a short lift!"

5   Handsome in a red-faced way, greying, medium of height, and dressed in a dark grey sport suit with a yellow-and-black flowered shirt, he said this in a nice, resonant, carrying voice which got the response of a scattering of **titters** from the bus. Esther, somewhat amused and

classifying him as a somatotonic[1], promptly forgot about him. And since she was sitting alone in the first regular seat, facing the back of the driver and the two front benches facing each other, she returned to looking out the window.

6 At the next stop, a considerable mass of people piled on and the last two climbing up were an elderly Oriental man and his wife. Both were neatly and somberly clothed and the woman, who wore her hair in a bun and carried a bunch of yellow and dark red chrysanthemums, came to sit with Esther. Esther turned her head to smile a greeting (well, here we are, Orientals together on a bus), but the woman was watching, with some concern, her husband who was asking directions of the driver.

7 His faint English was inflected in such a way as to make Esther decide he was probably Chinese, and she noted that he had to repeat his question several times before the driver could answer it. Then he came to sit in the seat across the aisle from his wife. It was about then that a man's voice, which Esther recognized soon as belonging to the somatotonic, began a loud **monologue** in the seat just behind her. It was not really a monologue, since he seemed to be addressing his seat companion, but this person was not heard to give a single answer. The man's subject was a figure in the local sporting world who had a nice fortune invested in several of the shining buildings the bus was just passing.

8 "He's as tight-fisted as they make them, as tight-fisted as they come," the man said. "Why, he wouldn't give you the sweat off his. . ." He paused here to rephrase his metaphor, "wouldn't give you the sweat off his palm!"

9 And he continued in this vein, discussing the private life of the famous man so frankly that Esther knew he must be quite drunk. But she listened with interest, wondering how much of this **diatribe** was true, because the

public legend about the famous man was **emphatic** about his charity. Suddenly, the woman with the chrysanthemums jerked around to get a look at the speaker and Esther felt her giving him a quick but thorough examination before she turned back around.

10 "So you don't like it?" the man inquired, and it was a moment before Esther realized that he was now directing his attention to her seat neighbor.

11 "Well, if you don't like it," he continued, "why don't you get off this bus, why don't you go back where you came from? Why don't you go back to China?"

12 Then, his voice growing **jovial**, as though he were certain of the support of the bus in this at least, he embroidered on this theme with a new **eloquence**, "Why don't you go back to China, where you can be **coolies** working in your bare feet out in the rice fields? You can let your pigtails grow and grow in China. Alla samee, mama, no tickee no shirtee. Ha, pretty good, no tickee no shirtee!"

13 He **chortled** with delight and seemed to be looking around the bus for approval. Then some memory caused him to launch on a new idea. "Or why don't you go back to Trinidad? They got Chinks[2] running the whole she-bang in Trinidad. Every place you go in Trinidad. . ."

[1]Somatotonic means an aggressive personality, associated with a muscular body.

[2]"Chinks" is an insulting term for Chinese people.

14   As he talked on, Esther, pretending to look out the window, felt the tenseness in the body of the woman beside her. The only movement from her was the trembling of the chrysanthemums with the motion of the bus. Without turning her head, Esther was also aware that a man, a mild-looking man with thinning hair and glasses, on one of the front benches, was smiling at the woman and shaking his head mournfully in sympathy, but she doubted whether the woman saw.

15   Esther herself, while believing herself properly annoyed with the speaker and sorry for the old couple, felt quite detached. She found herself wondering whether the man meant her in his **exclusion** order or whether she was identifiably Japanese. Of course, he was not sober enough to be interested in such fine distinctions, but it did matter, she decided, because she was Japanese, not Chinese, and therefore in the present case immune. Then she was startled to realize that what she was actually doing was **gloating** over the fact that the drunken man had specified the Chinese as the unwanted.

16   Briefly, there bobbled on her memory the face of an elderly Oriental man whom she had once seen from a streetcar on her way home from work. (This was not long after she had returned to Los Angeles from the concentration camp in Arkansas and been lucky enough to get a clerical job with the Community Chest.) The old man was on a concrete island at Seventh and Broadway, waiting for his streetcar. She had looked down on him benignly as a fellow Oriental, from her seat by the window, then been suddenly thrown for a loop by the legend on a large lapel button on his jacket. I AM KOREAN, said the button.

17   Heat suddenly rising to her throat, she had felt angry, then desolate and betrayed. True, reason had returned to ask whether she might not, under the circumstances, have worn such a button herself. She had heard rumors of I AM CHINESE buttons. So it was true then; why not I AM KOREAN buttons, too? Wryly, she wished for an I AM JAPANESE button, just to be able to call the man's attention to it, "Look at me!" But perhaps the man didn't even read English, perhaps he had been actually threatened, perhaps it was not his doing— his **solicitous** children perhaps had urged him to wear the badge.

18   Trying now to make up for her moral shabbiness, she turned towards the little woman and smiled at her across the chrysanthemums, shaking her head a little to get across her message (don't pay any attention to that stupid old drunk, he doesn't know what he's saying, let's take things like this in our stride). But the woman, in turn looking at her, presented a face so impassive yet cold, and eyes so expressionless yet hostile, that Esther's overture fell quite flat.

19   Okay, okay, if that's the way you feel about it, she thought to herself. Then the bus made another stop and she heard the man proclaim ringingly, "So clear out, all of you, and remember to take every last one of your slant-eyed pickaninnies[3] with you!" This was his final advice as he stepped down from the middle door. The bus remained at the stop long enough for Esther to watch the man cross the street with a slightly exploring step. Then, as it started up again, the **bespectacled** man in front stood up to go and made a clumsy speech to the Chinese couple and possibly to Esther. "I want you to know," he said, "that we aren't all like that man. We don't all feel the way he does. We believe in an America that is a melting pot of all sorts of people. I'm originally Scotch and French myself." With that, he came over and shook the hand of the Chinese man.

20   "And you, young lady," he said to the girl behind Esther, "you deserve a Purple Heart[4]

---

[3]"Pickaninnies" is an insulting term for children of slaves. It comes from the Spanish phrase: pequeños niños, "little children."

[4]A Purple Heart is a military honor for injury during battle.

or something for having to put up with that sitting beside you."

21   Then he, too, got off.

22   The rest of the ride was uneventful and Esther stared out the window with eyes that did not see. Getting off at last at the soldiers' home, she was aware of the Chinese couple getting off after her, but she avoided looking at them. Then, while she was walking towards Buro's hospital very quickly, there arose in her mind some words she had once read and let stick in her **craw**: People say, do not regard what he says, now he is in liquor. Perhaps it is the only time he ought to be regarded.

23   These words repeated themselves until her saving detachment was gone every bit and she was filled once again in her life with the infuri-atingly helpless, **insidiously** sickening sensation of there being in the world nothing solid she could put her finger on, nothing solid she could come to grips with, nothing solid she could sink her teeth into, nothing solid.

24   When she reached Buro's room and caught sight of his welcoming face, she ran to his bed and broke into sobs that she could not control. Buro was amazed because it was hardly her first visit and she had never shown such weakness before, but solving the mystery handily, he patted her head, looked around smugly at his roommates, and asked tenderly, "What's the matter? You've been missing me a whole lot, huh?" And she, finally drying her eyes, sniffed and nodded and bravely smiled and answered him with the question, yes, weren't women silly?

After You Read

Comprehension

1. Who is Esther Kuroiwa?

2. Why is she on the Wilshire bus?

3. When does Esther first think about being Japanese? Why does she think about it?

4. Why does Esther refer to her own behavior as "moral shabbiness"?

5. How did Esther try to make up for her behavior?

6. What effect did World War II have on Esther's family?

7. How did Esther's husband react to her arrival?

Analysis

1. Why is this story called "Wilshire Bus"?

2. What is the main idea in this story?

3. Why do you think the Chinese woman reacted as she did?

4. Why did Esther avoid looking at the Chinese couple when they got off the bus?

5. Esther thought: "People say, do not regard what he says, now he is in liquor. Perhaps it is the only time he ought to be regarded." What does this mean? Do you agree?

Vocabulary Building

Write the correct word in the blanks below. Each word is used once.

diatribe	jovial	solicitous
eloquence	monologue	unmitigated
emphatic	pastoral	vicarious
exclusion		

1. I got a(n) ——————— thrill from watching the action movie—I wish I were a stuntman.

2. The comedian gave a hilarious ———————.

3. She behaved in a(n) ——————— manner: she was very kind and concerned.

4. The setting was ———————the green farmland stretched out for miles.

5. The party was a(n) ——————— disaster: everyone arrived late, and the cake was terrible!

6. He is a ——————— man; he enjoys telling jokes and being happy.

7. With the ——————— of Ami, all of my friends are in my English class.

8. Her tone was ———————; she really wanted to go to the movies at 8:00, not 10:00.

9. She speaks with great ———————.

10. He began his long ——————— against the new law for the fifth time.

PUTTING IT ALL TOGETHER

In this chapter, you learned:

- to identify the purpose for your reading.
- to organize a study group.
- to summarize a reading's main points.

Use those skills as you do the following activities.

Read More

Find an article in a newspaper, magazine, or on the Internet that addresses immigration. Try to find an article that uses charts or graphs to give additional information. Read the article, then write in your journal about it. Discuss some of these ideas:

- Ideas in the article that interested you
- Parts that confused you
- How the story in the article relates to your life, or the life of someone you know

Then, report to your class about the article you found.

Write

Think back to your first day in a foreign country. Make a list of all of the impressions you can remember. Using your list, write a short essay describing what you saw, how you felt, and what you did. (If you have never traveled outside of your country, write about someone who immigrated to your country.)

Debate

Melting Pot or Mosaic?

The U.S. and Canada have often been called melting pots, places where different cultures blend into one culture. Others see them as mosaics, that is, places where many different cultures fit together, but each keeps its own characteristics.

Which image do you think is more accurate? Review the readings in this chapter to find support for your opinion. In a group of six, divide into two smaller groups each taking one side. Present arguments for your opinion. Each side should have the same amount of time to make their presentations.

CHECK YOUR PROGRESS

On a scale of 1 to 5, rate how well you have mastered the goals set at the beginning of the chapter:

1 2 3 4 5   identify and understand different purposes for reading.

1 2 3 4 5   organize a study group.

1 2 3 4 5   summarize a reading's main points.

1 2 3 4 5   recognize and understand compound words.

1 2 3 4 5   ask questions to get information you need about tests.

1 2 3 4 5   (your own goal)_____

1 2 3 4 5   (your own goal)_____

If you've given yourself a 3 or lower on any of these goals:

- visit the *Tapestry* web site for additional practice.
- ask your instructor for extra help.
- review the sections of the chapter that you found difficult.
- work with a partner or study group to further your progress.

L ook at the photo. Then discuss these questions with your
classmates:

- Should street signs and other public information be printed
  in different languages? Why or why not?
- Do you think it's easy to learn a new language?
- What new language would you like to learn to speak?

3

ALL TALK: LANGUAGE

A ll people speak some type of language; many people speak more than one. In this chapter, you will read about the political and social issues surrounding the subject of languages.

Setting Goals

In this chapter you will learn how to:

- scan a reading for specific information.

- expand your reading experience.

- draw inferences from your reading.

- understand connotations and denotations.

- reduce your anxiety about taking tests.

What other goals do you have for this chapter? Write one or two of them here.

_____

_____

◆ **Getting Started**

This chapter looks at different aspects of reading. Read these titles:

- "Sparring Over English Only," a newspaper article by Liz Willen
- "The Role of Language," a definition by D. Guice Longman, R. Holt Atkinson, and J. A. Breeden
- "Baby's Ears Pick Up Adult Language," an article by Paul Recer
- "Canada Loses Its French Accent," a newspaper article by Barbara Borst

1. Predict the ideas that this chapter will cover. List them here.

   _____

   _____

   _____

2. What do you already know about language in Canada?

   _____

   _____

   _____

3. What do you already know about "English Only" laws?

   _____

   _____

   _____

4. Do you know what an inference is? Explain it here. (If you don't know, make a guess.)

   _____

   _____

   _____

5. Look ahead at the pictures and charts in this chapter. What do these tell you about the topic of the chapter?

   _____

   _____

   _____

6. What do you want to learn from this chapter? Write down two questions you have about language.

_____

_____

_____

ACADEMIC POWER STRATEGY

Expand your reading experience to become a better reader. What does it mean to be a good reader? Does it mean that you read your assignments successfully and understand them? Does it mean you read quickly and with understanding? Or does it mean more than that?

Good readers read a lot, and they read a variety of texts: from the back of a cereal box to the business pages of the newspaper. Here are some reasons for reading different materials which you may not have thought of:

- Reading the front page of the **newspaper** may give you facts and ideas for writing in your courses.

- Reading a **cereal box** will tell you about your own nutritional habits.

- Reading a **business magazine** will tell you what kinds of jobs are available.

- Reading **comics** will teach you slang and what is considered funny in a culture.

- Reading a **novel** will give you pleasure.

When you read different types of materials, you start to see connections: between your biology class and what you ate for breakfast, between a novel you read and a lecture your English teacher gave, between a television show you watched and a magazine article. When you read widely, you read for personal growth.

(continued on next page)

Apply the Strategy

A. What other things can you think of to read? List them here:

_____

_____

_____

B. Take this quiz to find out what kind of reader you are. Be honest in your answers!

1. How many books have you read from cover to cover? (either fiction or nonfiction; don't count children's books)

   a. none   c. 3–5

   b. 1 or 2   d. more than 5

2. How often do you read the newspaper in any language?

   a. never   c. once or twice a week

   b. once or twice a month   d. three or more times a week

3. How many magazines do you read every month?

   a. none   c. 3–5

   b. one or two   d. more than five

4. How often do you read comics?

   a. never   c. once or twice a week

   b. once or twice a month   d. three or more times a week

5. How much reading do you do for your courses?

   a. 0–10 pages per week   c. 50–100 pages per week

   b. 10–50 pages per week   d. more than 100 pages per week

6. How do you feel about reading? Choose the sentence that best describes your thoughts.

   a. I hate reading!

   b. I read when I have to, and sometimes I enjoy it, but not often.

   c. I like to read, though I don't read much except assignments.

   d. I love to read! I read whenever I can.

7. Imagine you are participating in an experiment. You will spend one week in a room alone, and you must choose one of these options:

a. a television, VCR, video games, and a lot of videos; you will be paid $25

b. a television and some magazines to read; you will be paid $100

c. some newspapers, some books, and a radio; you will be paid $200

d. some newspapers, magazines, and books; you will be paid $500

Which would you choose?

Score:

Give yourself 0 points for every "a" you chose, 1 point for every "b", 2 points for every "c" and 3 points for every "d." Here is what your scores mean:

18–21 You are a reader who loves variety and loves to read! Keep up the good work.

14–17 You are a dedicated reader; work on bringing even more variety into your reading experience.

10–13 You are an experienced reader, but should add some more variety to your reading.

Below 10 You need to introduce yourself to different kinds of reading; this will both enrich your life and make you a better student.

◈Getting Ready to Read   Vocabulary Check

Which of these words and phrases do you already know? Check them off. Work with a partner to find the meanings of new words. Use a dictionary, if necessary. Add any new words you learn to your Vocabulary Log.

Mandarin Chinese is spoken by one billion people worldwide. It has the largest number of speakers of any language.

_____ amendment   _____ every nook and cranny

_____ assimilate   _____ punitive

_____ curtail   _____ resolution

_____ designate   _____ shrug off

> **Beowulf** is the oldest English epic, written in the 8th Century.

Reading Focus: Strategy Practice

In Chapter 1 (p. 5), you learned about active reading. Practice your marking scheme with the following reading passage.

 Read

Reading 1: Sparring Over English Only

by Liz Willen

1 Enraging fellow council members, two Queens[1] Republicans yesterday called for an **amendment** that would **designate** English as the country's official language.

2 Asking the council to do what Congress resisted, Councilmen Thomas Ognibene of Middle Village and Al Stabile of Ozone Park said the amendment is needed to create "a truly unified nation."

3 The amendment was immediately attacked and rejected by council members, who likened Ognibene to the television character Archie Bunker[2] and called him everything from wrongheaded to anti-immigrant. In addition, Council Speaker Peter Vallone (D-Astoria[3]) insisted that the resolution will never pass.

[1]Queens is a borough, or area, of New York City.

[2]Archie Bunker was a character on the television series, "All in the Family." He was known for being outspoken and bigoted.

[3]This is a typical designation of political party and location in newspaper writing. "D" refers to the Democratic party and "R" refers to the Republican party. "Astoria" indicates the area that the person represents.

4   "This resolution is DOA[4]," Vallone said. "It has already died once in this council, and I can assure you it will die again."

5   It was unclear what, if any, practical effect the resolution would have had, although about two dozen states have enacted such bills in recent years. Ognibene insisted it would force immigrants to learn English, and perhaps **curtail** bilingual education programs in the city's public schools.

6   "I am simply saying if we are going to have a society where people can grow and learn and **assimilate**, you have to have a common language ability to communicate," he said.

7   The debate turned the council's sleepy staid meeting into a battleground, and Ognibene was repeatedly asked to withdraw the **resolution**.

8   "Why do you need to open these wounds?" asked Councilman Guillermo Linares (D-Manhattan), who called the proposal "disgraceful and shameful . . . it is a total disrespect to all who acknowledge and embrace the richness and greatness of our language diversity."

9   Councilwoman Helen Marshall (D-Elmhurst) said the thousands of new immigrants who live in her district are extremely anxious to learn English.

10   "I cannot get enough classes . . . we are trying **every nook and cranny**," she said, describing efforts to get more classroom space for new immigrants. She called Ognibene's resolution "extremely **punitive** and contrary to everything the city stands for."

11   Ognibene **shrugged off** the criticism, and said any new immigrants who resist it "are insecure and take it as an insult, when it simply isn't so. Their lack of success . . . is a failure to learn the language."

◆ After You Read

Comprehension

1. What is the proposed amendment?

2. Who opposes the amendment? Why?

3. Who is in favor of the amendment? Why?

4. How many states have such amendments?

5. What is Councilwoman Marshall's opinion?

6. How did Ognibene feel about the criticism?

TUNING IN: "Ragin' Cajuns"

© CNN

Watch the CNN video about "Ragin' Cajuns." Discuss these questions with your class:

- Who are the Cajuns?

- How are Cajuns maintaining their language?

- What is the advantage of the new program to Cajun families?

[4]DOA means "dead on arrival." It is a term that originated in hospital emergency rooms, but now has come to mean anything that has failed before it has been through a process.

Analysis

Review your marks and comments on the reading. Then, in your *reading journal*, write your reaction to "Sparring Over English Only." In particular, write about your opinion of "English Only" laws. Should English be the "official language" of the U.S.?

Vocabulary Building

Choose the word from the list that belongs in each of the blanks. Write them in. You may have to change the form of some words (for example, make them plural or past tense).

assimilate	DOA	resolution
curtail	every nook and cranny	shrug off
designate	punitive	

1. Our committee wrote a _____ to change the rule.

2. It's not easy to _____ insults; they hurt people's feelings.

3. The amendment was _____. There was no way that the committee would even consider it.

4. They needed to _____ someone to direct the meeting since the president was absent.

5. Finally, they _____ the discussion of the issue; they had listened for over two hours.

6. Many immigrants find it difficult to _____ into a new culture.

7. They looked in _____ for a new room for their meetings.

8. The judge's decision was _____; he gave the speeder a fine of $100.

Getting Ready to Read

LANGUAGE LEARNING STRATEGY

Learn how to draw inferences in order to understand your reading better, and to be able to respond to it more accurately. An inference is an expectation about something you don't know directly, based on information you have. It is similar to a guess or prediction.

Inferences are affected by circumstances, by interpretations, and by assumptions you make.

First, think about how *circumstances* can affect your inferences. For example, imagine you are in a biology class and the teacher announces there will be a quiz. You will infer that the quiz will be about biology, not history or English (even though the teacher didn't say directly what it would be about!). If the teacher announces the quiz loudly and angrily, you might infer that that your teacher is giving the quiz because the class hasn't studied enough, or the teacher is angry with the students for some reason.

Your own beliefs affect the inferences you make, too. For example, if you believe biology is the hardest class you have, you might infer that the test will be extremely hard.

Language also plays an important role in inferences. The writer can lead the reader to certain inferences through word choice.

Apply the Strategy

In order to understand the role of language in inferences, read the following short article called "The Role of Language." As you read, consider where you are getting your inferences. Are they coming from the general context or background given in the article? From your own experience or beliefs? From the word choice in the sentence?

Vocabulary Check

Which of these words do you already know? Check them off. Work with a partner to find the meanings of new words. Use a dictionary, if necessary. You can add any new words you learn to your Vocabulary Log.

_____ congregation   _____ evoke   _____ rendition

_____ corsage   _____ flighty

 Read

Reading 2: The Role of Language

by Debbie Guice Longman, Rhonda Holt Atkinson, and Julie Ann Breeden

1 An eighty-eight-year-old woman attending church on Mother's Day was given a **corsage** by the minister for being the oldest mother in attendance. As he pinned the corsage on her, he said to the **congregation**, "Isn't it wonderful that this woman is so old." Reaching for his

microphone, she replied, "I'm not so old. I've just been here a long time."

2   In this example, word choice and assumptions that individuals hold about those words affect their inferences. The minister's and mother's statements were essentially the same. Their choice of words, however, carried different emotional reactions, or *connotation*. Words often have two types of meaning: *denotation* and connotation. Denotation refers to the actual dictionary definition of the word, without the attachment of an emotional response. For example, if you look up the word *aggressive*, you will find that it means "characterized by unprovoked offensive attacks, hostile behavior, vigorously energetic, and boldly assertive." If used to describe a type of treatment for a deadly disease, *aggressive* carries a positive emotional response. On the other hand, if your friend complains that a salesperson is aggressive, the picture you get of that salesperson is not necessarily positive. Thus, the word *aggressive* **evokes** both positive and negative emotions depending on the context in which the word is used. Your connotations for words become part of your assumptions and thus influence your inferences.

3   Writers and speakers consciously use connotative language to shape your inferences. They do this by choosing words with universal connotations. Thus, they expect you to respond emotionally in a certain way to the word choice. For example, imagine yourself in an art history class where the instructor is discussing some of the later paintings by the impressionist Claude Monet. The instructor carefully avoids including opinions about Monet because he wants his students to learn to evaluate paintings for form and style. However, in commenting on a later Monet painting, he says that "the apparently random choice of reds and oranges is a departure from the more serene blues and greens that Monet used in earlier paintings of the same scene." The use of the words *random* and *serene* helps you infer that he is not as impressed with Monet's later paintings as he is with the earlier ones. *Random*, when used to refer to an artist's color choice, has a more negative connotation. Since color is a prime element in painting, you would expect some sort of plan from a master painter. On the other hand, *serene* holds a more positive connotation. Word choice, then, helps you infer something about the instructor's opinion. Suppose the instructor really preferred Monet's later painting. In this case, his comment might have been, "By incorporating reds and oranges in his **rendition** of this scene, Monet makes a bold and dramatic departure from the conventional color combinations of his earlier works." Here the words *bold* and *dramatic* have a positive connotation, while the word *conventional* suggests something less than original.

4   More importantly, language affects the inferences you make without your even knowing it. This occurs when a speaker or writer either consciously or unconsciously uses words to influence your opinion. By choosing a word such as **flighty** rather than *flexible*, a speaker or writer paints a picture of something irresponsible rather than someone willing to change directions. Thus, making inferences about a situation involves careful examination of the word choices within the situation to see how they influence the predictions you make.

 **After You Read**

Comprehension

1. What is a connotation? Give an example.

_____

_____

2. What is a denotation? Give an example.

_____

_____

3. Give an example of a word that has both positive and negative connotations.

_____

_____

4. How do connotations affect our understanding of a speaker or writer?

_____

_____

Getting Ready to Read

LANGUAGE LEARNING STRATEGY

*S*can a reading for specific information to locate important facts quickly. Scanning means reading quickly to find specific information. Scanning for information can help you to remember and review important information from your reading.

When you scan, you should keep your eyes moving quickly, and search for only the information in the questions. Look at important words in the questions, and read especially for those words.

Apply the Strategy

Before you read the next article, scan the next reading for the following information and write the information below:

At what age do babies start hearing and remembering words?

_____

How did the experimenters test the babies' knowledge?

_____

How long did the experimenters wait to test the babies?

_____

(continued on next page)

Where will this research be published?

_____

_____

What conclusion did the experimenters draw?

_____

_____

Vocabulary Check

Which of these words and phrases do you already know? Check them off. Work with a partner to find the meanings of new words. Use a dictionary, if necessary. Add any new words you learn to your vocabulary log.

_____ cradle   _____ segment (verb)   _____ attend to

 Read

Reading 3: Baby's Ears Pick Up Adult Language

by Paul Recer

1 Better watch your language around the **cradle**. Babies as young as 8 months can hear and remember words—good and bad—researchers have discovered. "Little ears are listening," says Peter W. Jusczyk of Johns Hopkins University.

2 Jusczyk said new research shows that reading to children at such an early age, even if they don't seem to understand, can start the process of learning language.

3 "As you are sitting there reading, the child is learning something about sound patterns of words," he said. "That is important because they learn how words are formed and it helps them to **segment** sound patterns out of speech."

4 The conclusion is based on experiments in which infants listened repeatedly to three recorded stories. Two weeks later, the babies' recognition of words from those stories was compared against words that were not in the stories. Jusczyk said it was clear the infants recognized the story words.

5 A report on the study will be published Friday in the journal **Science.**

6 "This is important work," said Robin S. Chapman, a language-learning researcher at the University of Wisconsin, Madison. "It advances the findings of earlier work that showed children do **attend to** the sounds of language . . . and pick out those that are familiar."

7 She said the studies show that "a lot of language learning is happening in the first year of life. It shows that parents should talk to their children and the children will learn about the language from that talk."

◆ **After You Read**

Comprehension

1. What does the research with babies show about their language?

2. Describe the experiment that was conducted.

3. What assumptions do most people have about babies and language?

4. How does this article challenge those assumptions?

Test-Taking Tip

If you reduce your anxiety about taking tests, you will become a more effective test taker. You can eliminate some of your anxiety by writing. For example, to gain confidence, you could write about your greatest success in school. Write about how you felt when you did well. Or, to help you relax, you could write about the most relaxing place you know and describe how you feel when you are there. Writing about pleasant memories will help you relax and will take the focus off your anxiety.

◆ **Getting Ready to Read**

Look at the map of Canada. Circle the names of the provinces and cities you have heard of.

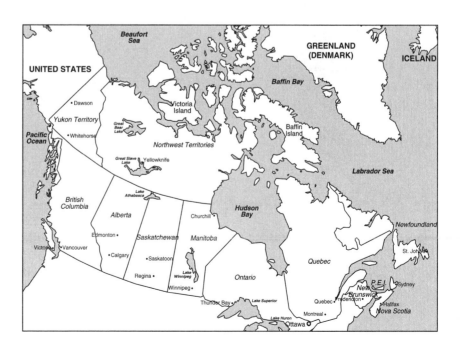

Vocabulary Check

Which of these words do you already know? Check them off. Work with a partner to find the meanings of new words. Use a dictionary, if necessary. You can add any new words you learn to your Vocabulary Log.

_____ cherish   _____ missionaries   _____ vitality

_____ elusive   _____ prairie   _____ vulnerable

_____ francophone   _____ province   _____ warrant

_____ heritage   _____ trappers

◈ Read

Reading 4: Canada Loses Its French Accent

by Barbara Borst

1   Aimé Gauthier knows the odds against keeping French alive on the Canadian **prairie**. His wife's sister and two brothers have largely abandoned their native tongue, even in their homes. Gauthier and his wife, Lucie, are proud to have raised four French-speaking children who now send their own children to public schools controlled by the **francophone** community.

2   The Gauthiers also are fluent in English—a necessity in the **province** of Manitoba, where French-speakers are just 2.3 percent of the population. But they **cherish** the **heritage** of the French explorers, **trappers** and **missionaries** who were the first colonists in this region.

3   "They have been saying for a long time that we were going to disappear," Gauthier said. "The more they take things away from us, the more we fight."

4   The Gauthiers are part of the larger struggle for cultural survival among French Canadians—outnumbered almost 4-to-1 by English-speakers in Canada, by 40-to-1 in North America. Of the 6.3 million Canadians whose native tongue is French, only 600,000 live outside Quebec.

5   Although Canada has two official languages—French and English—it is not a bilingual country. Only about 16 percent of Canadians can speak both languages well. It is, as many Canadians say, a land of "two solitudes," two peoples who hardly understand one another.

6   The Official Languages Act of 1969 commits the Canadian government to offering services in both French and English, where numbers **warrant**, and to enhancing the **vitality** of French—and English-speaking communities where they are in the minority.

7   Under the law, package labels across Canada are in both languages, and government agencies try to have a French-speaker available. Telephone calls in French to health, tax and police agencies in

> There are 74 million native speakers of French in the world. Another 52 million speak it as a second or other language.

Manitoba—including a branch of the Royal Canadian Mounted Police—all ended with a French-speaking employee on the line.

8   But Gauthier said he and other francophones often resort to English in face-to-face encounters at government offices.

9   "If you ask for service in French, they treat you like a trouble-maker," he said. "Everybody speaks English, so why do you have to ask for French?"

10   Victor Goldbloom, commissioner of official languages, says providing services in both languages remains "an **elusive** goal."

11   Minority language communities feel "more, not less, **vulnerable** and threatened," he said.

CANADIANS WHO SPEAK FRENCH AT HOME, WITH PERCENTAGE OF POPULATION		
Area	Number	Percent of total population
Canada	6,290,000	23.3
Quebec	5,660,000	83.0
Ontario	318,000	3.2
New Brunswick	223,000	31.2
Manitoba	25,000	2.3
Nova Scotia	22,000	2.5
Alberta	20,000	0.8
British Columbia	15,000	0.4
Saskatchewan	7,000	0.7
Prince Edward Island	3,000	2.4
Newfoundland	1,000	0.2

After You Read

Scan the reading and supply the following information. The first answer is done for you.

1. Percentage of people who speak French in Manitoba   _____2.3%_____

2. The first colonists in Manitoba   _____

3. The ratio of English speakers to French speakers in North America

     _____

4. The number of Canadians who speak French as a native language

     _____

5. Percentage of Canadians who speak both French and English well

     _____

6. The year the "Official Languages Act" was put into effect

     _____

Comprehension

1. Who are the Gauthiers?

2. Canada has two official languages, but is not considered a bilingual country. Why not?

3. Where do most French speakers live in Canada?

4. What was the effect of the Official Languages Act?

5. What does the phrase "a land of two solitudes" mean?

6. How does Mr. Gauthier feel about getting help from government offices in French?

Vocabulary Building

Complete the sentences below, showing you know the meanings of the words in **bold** type.

1. A **prairie** _____

2. My **heritage** _____

3. I **cherish** _____

4. _____ doesn't **warrant** my attention.

5. _____ is **elusive** to me.

6. _____ are **vulnerable** to _____.

7. _____ and _____ are Canadian **provinces**.

PUTTING IT ALL TOGETHER

In this chapter, you learned to scan a reading for specific information, how to make inferences in your reading, and the differences between connotations and denotations.

Use these new skills and strategies to do the next activity. Look at the comic strip, "Fox Trot":

Complete the chart regarding the inferences you can make:

Information	Inference
The boy's (Jason's) teacher assigned a 100-page book.	
The book has small type.	
The book doesn't have many illustrations.	
The girl thinks the assignment is due in a month.	
Jason says, "Oh fine, give me a heart attack," when he hears this.	

Read More

Find an article in a newspaper, magazine, or on the Internet that talks about an issue or political situation that relates to language learning. Read the article, then write in your *reading journal* about it. Discuss some of these ideas:

- ideas in the article that interested you.

- parts that confused you.

- how this story relates to your life, or to someone you know.

Then, report to your class about the article you found.

Discuss

1. Do you think it's easy or difficult to learn a foreign language? Explain.

2. Should countries have laws about language use? Why or why not?

3. Do you think people should fight to save languages that are "dying"? Why or why not?

4. What other question do you want to ask about language policies? Write it here and ask your classmates:

_____

Write

Choose one of these topics to write about:

1. Write a letter to your teacher about your progress in English. What aspects of the language are easiest for you? What aspects are difficult?

2. Does your home country have language policies? Write a short essay and explain what you know about language use in your country.

3. What are the advantages of being bilingual? Write an essay in which you explain the advantages and disadvantages of speaking more than one language.

CHECK YOUR PROGRESS

On a scale of 1 to 5, rate how well you have mastered the goals set at the beginning of the chapter:

1 2 3 4 5   scan a reading for specific information.

1 2 3 4 5   expand your reading experience.

1 2 3 4 5   draw inferences from your reading.

1 2 3 4 5   understand connotations and denotations.

1 2 3 4 5   reduce your anxiety about taking tests.

1 2 3 4 5   (your own goal)_____

1 2 3 4 5   (your own goal)_____

If you've given yourself a 3 or lower on any of these goals:

- visit the *Tapestry* web site for additional practice.
- ask your instructor for extra help.
- review the sections of the chapter that you found difficult.
- work with a partner or study group to further your progress.

L ook at the photos. Then discuss these questions with your classmates:

• Do you think there is too much food in your culture, or not enough?

• Do you think you have a good diet?

• Why do you think some people eat too much?

FOOD FOR THOUGHT: NUTRITION

What is the best diet? Which country enjoys the healthiest food? Surprisingly, the richest countries may not have the best diets. This chapter looks at diet, health, and the eating habits of different cultures.

Setting Goals

In this chapter you will learn how to:

◈ use comparisons and contrasts in reading.

◈ increase your reading speed to finish work faster and increase comprehension.

◈ manage your time to accomplish your assignments more efficiently.

◈ organize your notes for a test.

What other goals do you have for this chapter? Write two more in the blanks.

_____

_____

◆ Getting Started

This chapter looks at food and dietary habits. Read these titles:

- "Do You Eat Smart?" a quiz from the *Los Angeles Times*
- "America Weighs In," a research article by Shannon Dortch
- "A Pyramid of Health," an article by Daniel Rogov

What is food to one man may be fierce poison to others.

—LUCRETIUS (95–55 B.C.E.),
DE RARUM NATURA

1. Based on these titles, predict the ideas this chapter will cover. List them here. _____

   _____

   _____

2. What do you already know about healthy eating? _____

   _____

   _____

3. What kind of diet does your home country have? _____

   _____

   _____

4. Look ahead at the pictures and charts in this chapter. What do these tell you about the topic of the chapter? _____

   _____

   _____

5. What do you want to learn from this chapter? Write down two questions you have about food and diet. _____

   _____

   _____

TUNING IN: "Istanbul Dining"

Watch the CNN video about Istanbul dining. Discuss these questions with your class:

- What kinds of food are served in Istanbul?
- Describe what mealtimes are like in Istanbul.
- How does the Turkish style of eating compare with the style of eating in your native culture?

◆ Getting Ready to Read

In your journal, write about your diet. Do you think you have a good or a poor diet? What are your favorite foods? What foods could you not live without?

Vocabulary Check

Which of these words and phrases do you already know? Check them off. Work with a partner to find the meanings of new words and phrases. Use a dictionary, if necessary. Add any new words you learn to your vocabulary log.

_____ bagel	_____ on track	_____ sparingly
_____ legumes	_____ pita	_____ to go easy on
_____ mozzarella	_____ skimp	

◆ Read

Reading 1: Do You Eat Smart?

Los Angeles Times

Think about your typical eating pattern and food decisions.
Do you . . .

1. Consider nutrition when you make food choices?

   ☐ Usually   ☐ Sometimes   ☐ Never

2. Try to eat regular meals (including breakfast) rather than skip or **skimp** on some?

   ☐ Usually   ☐ Sometimes   ☐ Never

3. Choose nutritious snacks?

   ☐ Usually   ☐ Sometimes   ☐ Never

4. Try to eat a variety of foods?

   ☐ Usually   ☐ Sometimes   ☐ Never

5. Include new-to-you foods in meals and snacks?

   ☐ Usually   ☐ Sometimes   ☐ Never

6. Try to balance your energy (calorie) intake with your physical activity?

   ☐ Usually   ☐ Sometimes   ☐ Never

Now for the details. Do you . . .

7. Eat at least six servings* of grain products daily?

☐ Usually   ☐ Sometimes   ☐ Never

8. Eat at least three servings* of vegetables daily?

☐ Usually   ☐ Sometimes   ☐ Never

9. Eat at least two servings* of fruits daily?

☐ Usually   ☐ Sometimes   ☐ Never

10. Consume at least two servings* of milk, yogurt, or cheese daily?

☐ Usually   ☐ Sometimes   ☐ Never

11. **Go easy on** higher-fat foods?

☐ Usually   ☐ Sometimes   ☐ Never

12. Go easy on sweets?

☐ Usually   ☐ Sometimes   ☐ Never

13. Drink eight or more cups of fluids daily?

☐ Usually   ☐ Sometimes   ☐ Never

14. Limit alcoholic beverages (no more than one daily for a woman or two for a man)?

☐ Usually   ☐ Sometimes   ☐ Never

*Sample serving sizes

- Bread, cereals, rice and pasta group-six to 11 servings daily:

  1 slice (1 ounce) enriched or whole-grain bread

  $1/2$ hamburger roll, **bagel**, English muffin, or **pita**

  $1/2$ cup cooked rice or pasta

  1 ounce (1 cup) ready-to-eat cereal

- Milk, yogurt and cheese group—two to three servings daily:

  1 cup milk, buttermilk, or yogurt

  $1^1/_2$ ounces natural cheese (cheddar, **mozzarella**, Swiss)

  1 cup frozen yogurt

- Vegetable group-three to five servings daily:

  $1/2$ cup chopped raw, non-leafy vegetables

  $1/2$ cup cooked vegetables

  1 small baked potato (3 ounces)

  $3/_4$ cup vegetable juice

- Meat, poultry, fish, beans, eggs, and nuts group-two to three servings daily:

  2 to 3 ounces cooked lean meat, poultry, or fish

  $^1/_2$ cup cooked **legumes** (equals 1 ounce meat)

  1 egg (equals 1ounce meat)

- Fruit group—two to four servings daily:

  1 medium fruit (apple, orange, banana, peach)

  $^3/_4$ cup fruit juice

  $^1/_2$ cup canned, frozen or cooked fruit

- Fats, oils and sweets—use **sparingly**: sugars, salad dressings, oils, cream, butter, soft drinks

*Serving sizes vary depending on the food and food group.

Score Yourself

Usually = 2 points   Sometimes = 1 point   Never = 0 points

If you scored . . .

- **24 or more points:** Healthful eating seems to be your fitness habit already. Still, look for ways to stick to a healthful eating plan—and to make a "good thing" even better.

- **16 to 23 points:** You're **on track**. A few easy changes could help you make your overall eating plan healthier.

- **9 to 15 points:** Sometimes you eat smart—but not often enough to be your "fitness best." What might be your first steps to healthier eating?

- **0 to 8 points:** For your good health, you're wise to rethink your overall eating style. Take it gradually—step by step!

Whatever your score, take steps for healthful eating. Gradually turn your "nevers" into "sometimes" and your "sometimes" into "usuallys."

After You Read

Comprehension

1. How much liquid should you drink in a day?

2. Which foods should you eat only sparingly?

3. What foods should you eat the most of?

4. How much alcohol should you limit yourself to in a day?

◆ **Vocabulary Building**

Review the vocabulary for this reading. Then, match the word or phrase to its meaning. Draw a line from the word in column A to its meaning in column B.

A

1. economically
2. flat bread
3. to go easy on
4. round bread with a hole in the middle
5. type of cheese
6. bean
7. to be on track

B

a. bagel
b. legume
c. mozzarella
d. pita
e. skimp
f. sparingly
g. to do well

FoxTrot   by Bill Amend

FOXTROT © 1998 Bill Amend. Reprinted with permission of UNIVERSAL PRESS SYNDICATE. All rights reserved.

ACADEMIC POWER STRATEGY

Manage your time to finish your assignments more efficiently. Some days it probably seems like you will never get through all the things you have to do. How can you do it? Efficient students *manage their time* well. Many different tools exist for time management; it is helpful to find the one right for you.

Apply the Strategy

Here are three suggestions for time management. Choose the one you think will work best for you and try it for one week. If it doesn't work well, try another method.

1. Keep a "to do" list on a piece of paper. *Prioritize* the items on your list—put a "1" by the most important items, a "2" by the next important item, and so forth. Complete your list in order of importance of items.

2. Buy or make a weekly calendar. Write your assignments and other tasks down at the days and times they are due. Write reminders in your calendar about important upcoming dates. Take your calendar with you when you are at school or work so you can write things down when you hear about them. (This will keep you from forgetting later on.)

3. Buy or use an electronic calendar or "to do" list. Many computers come with software that helps you manage your time. If you have a computer, check to see what software it came with. Buy software for time management, or a hand-held electronic organizer.

◆ Getting Ready to Read

Reading Focus:
Previewing Titles and Subheadings

The following reading contains several subheadings. Previewing these subheadings will give you a good idea of what the article is about. This, in turn, will help you to understand the reading more as you read. Take a couple of minutes and preview the sub-headings in this reading. Write them here:

Article Title: _____ America Weighs In _____

Subheading 1: _____

Subheading 2: _____

Subheading 3: _____

Subheading 4: _____

Subheading 5: _____

Subheading 6: _____

Test-Taking Tip

Organize your notes in order to study more efficiently for tests. To get organized, the first thing you should do is make a list of all the things that will help you study: for example, your notes, some notecards, your textbook, your graded homework, and so forth. After you make your list, assemble all the things you'll use, and put them in one convenient location. Make special folders or labels to help you quickly identify the materials for your test. When you're ready to study, you'll have everything you need.

Body mass index (also called BMI) is a calculation of this formula: BMI = (704 × weight in pounds) divided by (height in inches × height in inches). If the result is more than 25, you are considered overweight.

Vocabulary Check

Which of these words do you already know? Check them. Work with a partner to find the meanings of new words. Use a dictionary, if necessary. Add any new words you learn to your Vocabulary Log.

_____ anorexia	_____ immutable
_____ baby boom	_____ per-capita
_____ caveat	_____ plummet
_____ cholesterol	_____ proxy
_____ chronic	_____ rudimentary
_____ corroborate	_____ sedentary
_____ emaciated	_____ spawn
_____ flab	

Read

Reading 2: America Weighs In

by Shannon Dortch

1 Americans enjoy the most abundant and varied diet in the world. Food is cheap, plentiful, and tasty. All those readily available nutrients should make us a strong, healthy people. But for an increasing share of U.S. adults, life in the land of plenty is making them plenty fat. The percent of adults aged 20 to 74 who are obese based on their body mass index increased from 24 percent in the 1960s to 33 percent in 1988–91. By 1994, the share of all adults aged 20 and older who are overweight climbed further, to 35 percent. Applying that rate to the adult population yields a total of 65 million U.S. adults aged 20 or older who were overweight in 1988–94. We don't get to blame the aging population, either. Overweight has become more prevalent among all age groups, not just the elderly.

2 Children and adolescents are following the example of their elders. The share of children aged 6 to 11 who are overweight increased from 11 percent in the late 1970s to 14 percent

in 1994. For children aged 12 to 17, the share doubled to 12 percent in 1994.

3   Overweight people create markets for large-sized clothing and weight-loss products and services. But Americans seem to be losing interest in weight-loss diets. One market that is certain to benefit from this trend is health care. The National Center for Health Statistics (NCHS) says that overweight and obese adults are at increased risk for numerous acute and **chronic** conditions, ranging from high blood pressure to diabetes to arthritis.

4   Most doctors believe that a wide range of chronic ailments can be prevented or mitigated by maintaining a reasonable body weight. Former Surgeon General[1] C. Everett Koop recently said that if he had stayed in office longer, "I would have launched the same assault on obesity that I did on smoking."

Plump, Overweight, or Obese

5   There are several different ways to measure the prevalence of overweight in the population. The NCHS uses body mass index (BMI) to determine if a person is overweight. BMI is a ratio of height to weight. "Overweight" means about 124 percent of desirable weight for men and 120 percent for women, after adjustments for clothing and shoes. Since obesity is defined as having a body weight at least 20 percent greater than desirable, BMI captures only obese children and adults.

6   People who could stand to lose a pound or two, and even some who should probably shed 10 or 20, are not counted as overweight using this measure. The standard height/weight tables produced by the Metropolitan Life Insurance Company aren't so forgiving. When you ask U.S. adults their height

and weight, and determine their overweight status based on the tables, the share who exceed their desirable body weight jumps to almost seven in ten in 1995. This is how *Prevention* magazine measured overweight for the 13 years it conducted the *Prevention* Index survey of Americans' health. *Prevention* said that the share of adults who are overweight by its definition increased from 58 percent in 1983 to 68 percent in 1995.

7   Many researchers believe BMI is the best way to determine overweight precisely because it captures the population most at risk of overweight-related health problems. In addition, the way BMI is determined by the NCHS makes it more reliable than self-reported data on weight. The temptation to understate your weight by a pound or ten is natural, and the tendency to underreport one's weight increases with extra pounds.

8   Participants in the NCHS's National Health and Nutrition Examination Survey (NHANES) didn't have that luxury. They were weighed in the presence of researchers while wearing a standardized gown and slippers. But even with the fudge factor[2] eliminated, overweight rates based on BMI are still lower than those based on MetLife tables, because BMI captures only the more seriously overweight.

9   Other surveys **corroborate** the findings of NHANES and the *Prevention* Index, which has obesity experts agreeing the trend is genuine. Overweight rates have increased across most age and race groups. Young adults aged 20 to 29, who presumably are among the most educated and physically active Americans, have seen their overweight rates increase steadily for women between 1960–62 and 1988–91, and remain stable for men.

10   Older adults may have assumed for years that old age was a license for weight gain. But

---

[1]The Surgeon General is appointed by the President of the United States, and is seen as the chief medical authority.

[2]"Fudge factor" refers to the number of pounds that people tend to understate their true weights.

some middle-aged and elderly groups have shown declines in prevalence of overweight over the 30-year period. Between the 1976–80 and 1988–91 NHANES surveys, rates declined for black women aged 50 to 59. They were virtually stable for black women aged 60 to 74. There was a marked decline in the percent of black men aged 40 to 49 who are overweight, but rates for white men and women either rose or were stable for all age groups. Researchers at the NCHS aren't patting Americans on the back for these decreases, however. Among middle-aged and older adults, drops in the share who are overweight probably relate to natural aging-related decreases in lean body mass. In addition, older overweight adults may simply be dying prematurely, which reduces their numbers in specific population groups.

11   For the most part, women are more likely than men to be overweight. There are some exceptions among non-Hispanic white females, who may identify more strongly than non-whites with societal ideals of slimness. Black women have the highest prevalence of overweight of all Americans, at almost half in 1988–91.

Living to Eat

12 There is only one way to get fat: we have to consume more food calories than we expend in activity. It's an **immutable** law of nature. Where researchers disagree is on the component of the formula that's making more Americans overweight. Are we eating more, are we less active, or is it a combination of the two? "There's very little evidence that we're increasing our intake," says David Levitsky, a professor of nutritional sciences and psychology at Cornell University. "The only thing that's changed is expenditures, and that's **plummeting**." By expenditures, Levitsky doesn't necessarily mean leisure-time fitness activities, such as jogging, aerobics, or tennis. Technological innovations from automobiles to TV remote controls allow us to burn fewer and fewer calories carry-ing on the activities necessary for everyday life. In addition, changes in our economy have resulted in fewer jobs that require high energy expenditures, and more where the only physical activity performed is walking to and from the water cooler. "It's difficult to expend energy, even if you want to," Levitsky says.

13   Americans aren't compensating for their relatively newfound energy savings by increasing recreational exercise. An annual study by the Centers for Disease Control shows that the share of adults who exercise was stable between 1985 and 1994. About 19 percent participated in regular sustained activity in 1994, and 11 percent participated in regular vigorous activity. Thirty-one percent were **sedentary**.

14   While researchers like Levitsky question whether increased calorie intake is contributing to the increasing prevalence of overweight, some recent data suggest we may be eating more, or at least eating foods that are more likely to be stored by the body as fat. One **caveat** about these nutrition data: they are self-reported, with researchers asking survey participants to recall what they've eaten over a 24-hour period. Respondents may underreport consumption of "bad" foods, or they may not remember exactly what they had.

15   The average daily calorie intake recorded by NHANES III for adults aged 20 to 74 was 2,200 in 1988–91, up from 1,969 for NHANES II in 1976–80. The average total number of fat grams consumed each day also increased, from 81 to 85.6. There was little change in the average percent of daily calories attributed to fat, at 34 percent in 1988–91.

16   Even with the recent reported increase in daily calories, the average American's diet still has less energy than it did at the beginning of the century, says Audrey Cross, a clinical professor and nutritionist in Columbia University's School of Public Health. Yet the activities of daily life are much less physically demanding. What researchers are now trying to determine is how differences in the types of foods we eat may be contributing to overweight.

17   "The form of our calories has changed," Cross says. At the beginning of the 20th century, the American diet was more dependent on fruits, vegetables, and grains—foods that are not refined. An adult eating the same number of calories as our forebears is bound to get more of them from refined food sources. "We consume more of our calories from fat, and more of those calories are from polyunsaturated[3] fats, which are refined from grains, such as corn," says Cross.

Burgers and Big Gulps[4]

18   Asking people what they ate in the past day is one way to assess the American diet. Another is to track the amount of food available for human consumption. The U.S. Department of Agriculture's Economic Research Service records food disappearance data as a **proxy** for consumption. It warns, however, that these data may overstate what is actually eaten, because they do not account for waste. But assuming that we aren't wasting more food per person than we did 20-odd years ago, it appears Americans are eating more of most foods—some that make us fat, and others that contribute to good health.

19   Some messages about good nutrition may be getting through. Average annual **per-capita** consumption of beef fell 14 percent between 1980–84 and 1990–94, to 63 pounds per person. As Americans heeded medical advice to cut back on dietary fat from red meat, their chicken consumption jumped 37 percent, to 46 pounds each. Yet beef remains our favorite type of meat.

20   Per-capita consumption of fruits and vegetables also rose over the period. The average American ate 121 pounds of fresh fruit per year in 1990–94, up 12 percent from ten years earlier. Fresh vegetable consumption rose 14 per-cent, to 169 pounds each. USDA officials expect all these healthful consumption patterns to continue into the next decade.

21   Other food disappearance trends show a less flattering side of the modern diet. Per-capita consumption of milk is down, while soft drinks are on the rise. Cheese, except for skim-milk-based products, is flying high; so are salty snack foods and sweeteners besides refined sugar. The reasons can be summarized in one word: convenience.

22   Eating away from home is more popular than ever, especially at fast-food restaurants. Per-capita consumption of frozen french fries now surpasses fresh potatoes. Most of these fries are eaten out. The average American consumed almost twice as much cheese in 1990–94 as 20 years earlier, at 25.7 pounds. (This excludes full-skim American, cottage, pot, and baker's cheeses.) Most of that extra cheese is going down in pizza restaurants and at home in convenience dishes like boxed scalloped potatoes and frozen broccoli and cheese.

23   Eating food on the run and munching salty snacks has been making Americans thirsty for bubbly refreshment. Per-capita consumption of non-diet soft drinks increased 13 percent between 1990 and 1994, to 40 gallons a year. That equates to 645 8-ounce servings a year, or just less than 2 soft drinks a day. In 1990, carbonated soft drinks accounted for 21 percent of the refined sugar consumed by the average U.S. resident.

24   Don't Americans know that eating immoderate quantities of french fries and pizza can lead to overweight? They appear to have at least a **rudimentary** understanding of the link between diet and health. More than nine in ten women who are the main meal preparers in their households know that there are health problems related to being overweight, according to the USDA's 1989–91 Diet and Health

---

[3]"Polyunsaturated" refers to a highly processed type of fat.

[4]A "Big Gulp" is a large-sized drink sold at the convenience store 7-Eleven.

Knowledge Survey. Almost 80 percent know that high fat intake may lead to health problems, 86 percent are aware that **cholesterol** can mean trouble, and 88 percent know that sodium may have negative effects on health.

Eating Culture

25 This leaves obesity researchers struggling with the questions of why we eat a lot of fat when we know it makes us fat. What's more, overweight is on the rise, even as popular culture continues to celebrate slimness, to the point of embracing **emaciated** fashion models as standards of female beauty.

26 A couple of different societal forces are pushing Americans toward overweight, even though we value slenderness, says Peter Stearns, a social historian and dean of the College of Humanities and Social Sciences at Carnegie Mellon University. First, broad changes have conspired to make many adults feel stressed at home and work, from corporate downsizing to being a single parent. "A number of people are saying, 'I do accept the slimness values, I know I'm violating them, but my life is hard enough,'" Stearns says. "They eat as a form of release. People are eating more because it's a form of gratification."

27 Second, Americans live in the only country in the world where pie-eating contests are old-fashioned fun, and all-you-can-eat restaurants dot the landscape, Stearns says. "We have a long national tradition of believing eating is a sign of personal, societal, and family well-being," he says. "There's no society that compares to ours in the importance and frequency of snacking. We show our prosperity through food; we give ourselves lifts by nibbling."

28 Many obesity experts believe that cultural standards of slenderness are primarily embraced by white Americans, to whom slimness becomes more important with increasing income. Yet blacks, particularly black women, don't necessarily buy into the slim-is-better philosophy. "African-American women were traditionally more important to the family—they were more likely to work," Stearns says. "They had stature in the family, and didn't have to resort to slimness to define their sexuality."

29 If there is greater acceptance of overweight among black women, it's unclear whether it promotes their higher-than-average rates of overweight or results from them. One thing is certain: this high prevalence of overweight among blacks is not genetic, says Cross of Columbia University. Obesity is not an issue for blacks native to Africa, she says. "But in first-generation African immigrants to the U.S., you see massive increases in obesity." The low household incomes of many blacks living in the U.S. may play a major role in their high levels of overweight. "If you're poor, you learn to eat foods that yield the greatest amount of energy for the lowest cost—that's fat," says Cornell University's Levitsky. "Poor people learn to eat foods that allow them to survive under conditions of scarcity."

Suffering for Nothing

30 Since people gain weight by eating more calories than they use, losing weight is a matter of eating fewer calories than the body needs for daily activities, increasing the amount of energy expended, or both. The approach of choice for most overweight adults is the first—going on a diet. Yet anyone who's tried dieting knows how difficult it is. Self-denial, especially where food is concerned, is practically un-American. That's one reason why diets almost always fail their practitioners. That doesn't keep overweight adults from trying diets, many over and over again. Their persistence fuels a huge industry of structured weight-loss programs, diet books, and talk-show tips.

31 The failure of weight-loss dieting to yield lasting results may be wearing on many Americans. The percent of both men and women who say they've been on a weight-loss diet in the past six months declined between 1986 and 1996. The share for men dropped to 8 per-

cent from 10 percent in 1986. The decline was more significant for women, dropping to 16 percent in 1996 from 20 percent ten years earlier, according to Mediamark Research of New York City.

32   Women are clearly the biggest dieters, perhaps because they feel more pressure from media images to conform to slimness ideals. However, younger women who are the targets of most fashion and cosmetic advertising are the very ones who are most losing faith in dieting. In 1996, 14 percent of women aged 18 to 24 were on a weight-loss diet, compared with 21 percent ten years earlier. The share also declined for 25- to-34-year-olds, to 18 percent from 25 percent in 1986.

33   "Young women are managing body image," says Rochelle Udell, editor-in-chief of *Self* magazine. "They've grown up in an environment where diet alone doesn't work. They've seen it with their mothers and aunts, and they've come to learn that you don't just restrict food to manage weight." *Self* devotes many pages of editorial copy to issues surrounding weight management and healthy body image with the aim of helping women broaden their perception of what constitutes a normal, attractive body. "We're concerned about women following unrealistic ideals of body image," Udell says. "I don't approve of obesity, and I don't approve of **anorexia** either. What matters is to be at a healthy weight for you." While there may be some backlash among young women to media images of thin models, it's unfair to blame slender women for the conflict many feel between the gratification of food and the quest for slenderness, Udell says. They are not the ones behind ever-expanding food portions, such as 72-ounce soft drinks and buckets of popcorn in movie theaters, and fast-food meals featuring super-sized burgers and fries. "It's an insidious problem," she says. "We're training people to eat these portions, because they perceive them as a good value."

34   Whether for the love of fast food or frustration with restricted eating, dieting rates may continue their ten-year pattern of decline. That would reduce the number of U.S. dieters from just fewer than 24 million in 1997, to 20 million in 2007. The number might decline further, if it weren't for the large **baby-boom** generation boosting the number of dieters among the middle-aged. It is possible that this appearance-conscious generation won't stand for extra **flab** or its associated health risks. Boomers could **spawn** a fresh outbreak of fitness-and-diet awareness. However, current obesity figures suggest otherwise. The prevalence of overweight has increased among boomer age groups, just as it has for most other Americans.

Obesity Tomorrow

35 The growing rates of overweight have public-health officials calling obesity an epidemic. Yet they haven't found a successful treatment for the problem. Some hope that new diet drugs, such as the recently approved Redux[5], will help people slim down. In the meantime, they're faced with a population that appears less restrained than ever in its food choices. In 1994, more than six in ten U.S. adults said they eat whatever they want, up from 45 percent in 1977, according to Roper Starch Worldwide. The next generation of adults is providing little hope for change. "My greatest concern is obesity in children, " says Judith Stern, a professor of nutrition and internal medicine at the University of California in Davis, who chaired the National Institutes of Medicine committee charged with evaluating weight-control methods. "They tell us the future."

36   What will help? Many experts, including former Surgeon General Koop, think a long-term

---

[5]Redux was found to cause heart problems, and is no longer available as a weight-control drug in the U.S.

solution may lie on the expenditure side of the weight-control equation. In December 1994, Koop founded Shape Up America!, a nonprofit educational campaign to encourage physical fitness. The organization has conducted surveys to identify barriers to activity and healthful eating, among other things.

37   One of the most difficult issues faced by obesity experts is how to motivate people to do what they know is best for them. Most Americans have a good idea of what foods may lead to overweight, especially now that new food-labeling laws are in effect. And they know that regular physical activity improves health. In a 1996 survey of adults aged 18 and older, 85 percent said they believe people who exercise regularly live longer than those who don't. Almost three-fourths say regularly exercisers are happier, and 71 percent say they are more attractive than non-exercisers, according to American Sports Data of Hartsdale, New York.

38   Reducing obesity rates may take a public-awareness campaign of the magnitude of government anti-smoking efforts. However, it seems unlikely that fast-food french-fries containers will ever have labels stating: "Warning: this food may endanger your health by making you overweight." Instead, public-health officials are hoping to get Americans off the couch and on the sidewalk, bicycle, or tennis court. "It's a conversation we haven't started on a mass level yet," says Cross, the Columbia University nutritionist. "People aren't resistant to exercise—they've just forgotten how to do it."

◆ **After You Read**

The biggest food crop in the U.S. is corn.

One McDonald's Big Mac and a large order of fries has 1,010 calories, over half of the calories needed by an average adult in a day.

Comprehension

1. What percentage of American adults were obese in the 1960s? In the 1980s?

2. How has children's weight changed?

3. What negative effects does overweight have?

4. How do you calculate BMI? Why is it considered a good measure of weight?

5. How do weight trends differ in different ethnic groups?

6. What is the cause of overweight, scientifically speaking?

7. How has the "form" of calories consumed by Americans changed?

8. In what ways has the American diet improved recently, according to the article?

9. Why don't more Americans exercise?

10. Why are many Americans overweight?

11. Why do fewer Americans go on weight-loss diets than before?

LANGUAGE LEARNING STRATEGY

Use comparisons and contrasts to help you better comprehend your reading. Writers often use comparisons and contrasts to present information. A comparison looks at the features that things have in common; a contrast looks at differences between things. These ideas provide a way for the reader to understand relationships and qualities of information. Understanding how a writer uses comparisons will help you understand the relationship between ideas in a reading.

Apply the Strategy

Review "America Weighs In." Look at the comparisons and contrasts that the writer uses. Complete the following table. The first example is done for you. Add a category of your own at the end of the list.

CATEGORY	SIMILARITIES	DIFFERENCES
1. men and women	both groups suffer from overweight	women are more overweight than men; women diet more than men do
2. minority groups and Caucasians		
3. past and current generations		
4. current and future generations		
5. people who exercise and those who don't		
6. _____		

◆**Vocabulary Building**

Many English words come from two ancient languages: Greek and Latin. These words are frequently used in "academic" types of writing. Look at the following words, taken from the reading. Match the word with the meaning of its root. The first one is done for you as an example. (G means the word comes from Greek, L from Latin.)

Word		Root and Meaning
1. anorexia	_e_	a. (G) *khron* = time
2. caveat	____	b. (G) *khol* = bile, gall; *stere* = stiff
3. cholesterol	____	c. (L) *cap* = head
4. chronic	____	d. (L) *maci* = leanness
5. corroborate	____	e. (G) *orexis* = appetite
6. emaciate	____	f. (L) *sede* = sit
7. immutable	____	g. (L) *miti* = mild, gentle
8. mitigate	____	h. (L) *muta* = change
9. per-capita	____	i. (L) *cave* = beware
10. sedentary	____	j. (L) *robora* = strengthen

◆**Getting Ready to Read**

The next reading examines different eating habits in different cultures. Before you read, discuss these questions with your class:

- Which cultures have the best diets, in your opinion?
- What kinds of foods keep you healthy?
- What kinds of exercise should you do to keep healthy?

Vocabulary Check

Which of these words do you already know? Work with a partner to find the meanings of new words. Use a dictionary, if necessary. Add any new words you learn to your Vocabulary Log.

_____ antioxidants	_____ conspicuous
_____ arteries	_____ coronary
_____ charismatic	_____ diabetes

_____ epidemiologists   _____ pinnacle

_____ genetics   _____ robust

_____ life expectancy   _____ temperament

_____ longevity   _____ volatile

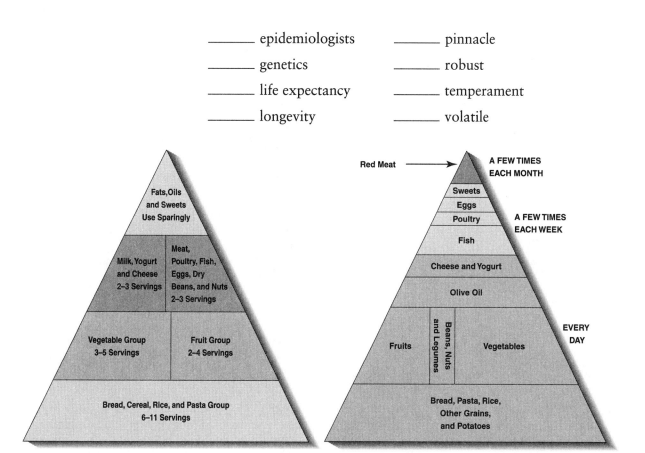

American food pyramid   Mediterranean food pyramid

LANGUAGE LEARNING STRATEGY

Increase your reading speed to finish your work faster and understand it better. It might surprise you to learn that if you read too slowly, you actually understand *less*, not *more* of what you read. One reason is that when you read slowly, you focus too much on individual words, and not the meaning of phrases and sentences. Also, when you read slowly, you often miss the main ideas, since you can forget them when concentrating on individual words.

Native speakers of English read about 250 words per minute when they read an essay or story. Of course, different kinds of reading have different demands, so that number is just an *average*. It is not always appropriate to read at that rate.

(continued on next page)

Apply the Strategy

The best way to learn to read more quickly is to practice. The next reading is split into two sections. Read the first section, timing your reading. Then, read the second, trying to improve your speed.

As you try to read more quickly, don't sacrifice understanding. Read at a comfortable pace, but don't pause on any one word or idea. Keep your eyes moving. If you don't know some of the words, don't stop to look them up. Just keep reading. You can review the passages or words you didn't understand after you finish.

◈**Read**

Reading 3: A Pyramid of Health

by Daniel Rogov

Starting Time: _____ : _____

Part I

1 In recent years a large number of medical specialists, nutritionists, and dieticians have devoted much effort to convincing us that just about everything we eat is bad for us. But now, if one accepts the findings of two recent international conferences held in San Francisco—one on the diets of the Mediterranean and the other on wine and health—there's some good news. Excellent health, increased **longevity**, and an abundance of the simple pleasures of life are all readily available if you're prepared to follow "the Mediterranean Diet," which is not so much a "diet" as a way of living.

2 Interest in the Mediterranean diet was first raised in the 1950s, when researchers from Harvard University's School of Nutrition became curious about why men and women on the islands of Crete and Sicily, many of whom lived well into their 80s, had one of the lowest rates of heart disease and cancer in the world.

3 They also noted a remarkably low rate of heart disease in other nations around the Mediterranean. In 1959, for example, the **coronary** heart-disease death rate for American men between the ages of 55 and 59 was eight times that of Greek men of the same age (748 per 100,000 for Americans versus 95 per 100,000 for Greeks).

4 Incidences of other diseases, such as breast and colon cancer, were also lower in the Mediterranean region, and in Greece and southern Italy **life expectancy** was about four years longer than in the U.S. or Northern Europe.

5 During more than 15 years of research, **epidemiologists**, who study large populations to identify "risk factors" for diseases, were unable to identify the crucial factors which affected the health of these Mediterranean populations. Finally, in 1964, the researchers began to focus on what they identified as the "traditional Mediterranean diet."

6 They noted that the core of traditional Mediterranean cuisine of the '50s and '60s was an abundance of fruits and vegetables as well as large quantities of bread, pasta, legumes, nuts, couscous[1], rice and other grains. The overall diet included very little meat and only moderate amounts of fish, poultry and dairy products. Sweets played a small role in the dining habits of the people and fruits were the main form of dessert. The two most **conspicuous** features of the Mediterranean diet were that olive oil accounted for as much as

---

[1]Couscous is a type of grain that is eaten with vegetables or meat.

40 percent of all of the fat consumed by most Mediterranean people and that they consumed wine with nearly every meal.

7   This and subsequent research resulted in the creation of the Optimal Traditional Mediterranean Diet Pyramid at the International Conference on the Diet of the Mediterranean. The pyramid consists of nine levels, each representing the stress to be placed on various elements of the diet.

8   Red meat, at the pyramid's **pinnacle**, is recommended only a few times per month. Sweets, poultry, eggs and fish are recommended a few times per week, and olives, olive oil, dairy products, beans, legumes, nuts, fruits and vegetables and whole grains, including pasta, rice, couscous, polenta and burghul[2], are recommended on a daily basis. The major focus at recent conferences has been on olive oil, nuts and wine.

9   According to Prof. Walter Willet, chairman of the Department of Nutrition at Harvard's School of Public Health, olives and olive oil lower levels of LDL, which is considered the harmful or "bad" cholesterol because it contributes to the buildup of fatty deposits in the **arteries**, thereby raising the risk of heart disease. Olive oil also helps the body maintain the level of HDL, the "good" cholesterol which removes such deposits.

10   According to Willet, olive oil also contains high quantities of **antioxidants**, today's nutritional miracle, and these are also thought to ward off heart disease. Perhaps best of all, according to Dr. R. Curtis Ellison, professor of Medicine and Public Health at Boston University, antioxidants can also prevent various cancers by neutralizing **volatile** chemicals that drift in the bloodstream.

11   As to the consumption of wine, the other major factor singled out for special attention at the conferences, the pyramid suggests that a moderate level of alcohol consumption, especially of red wine, also raises the HDL level and

lowers the risk of heart disease and reduces overall mortality.

12   There are a few potential problems in all of this. Some point out, for example, that advocating a diet in which nearly 40 percent of the calories we take in comes from olive oil is problematic. Olive oil is pure 100 percent fat, and fat, no matter what its positive effects may be, is public health enemy number one. In fact, some say the ideal fat intake should be no more than 10 percent of our daily intake.

13   In addition, since all fats, including olive oil, have nine calories per gram, it is important not to overdo them. If the Mediterranean diet results in significant weight gain, the value of the diet is undermined, for that would increase other risk factors, including high blood pressure and **diabetes**.

Enter your finishing time: _____ : _____ Total number of minutes spent reading: _____ Divide 831 by the number of minutes: _____ Your reading rate: _____ words per minute. How close are you to 250 words per minute? If you are close, try to maintain that pace. If you are still far below, try to read a little more quickly in Part II of the reading.

Starting Time: _____ : _____

Part II
·········

14   Israeli medical specialists and nutritionists are enthusiastic, but more moderate than their American colleagues, in their reactions to the concept of the Mediterranean Diet. Olga Raz, senior nutritionist at Ichilov Hospital, feels that although "the pyramid can serve as a general guideline, one has to think of an entire lifestyle, one that includes factors such as exercise and stress management, and not merely of one or two dietary factors."

[2]Polenta is ground corn, cooked in water. Burghul is another name for bulgur, a type of grain.

15   Raz also points out that studies of the Mediterranean diet have ignored factors of **genetics** and, because of the bias in sampling techniques[3], are far more applicable to men than women.

16   Some object to the pyramid, claiming that it has never been representative of the real Mediterranean diet. On a recent visit, cookbook writer Claudia Roden questioned whether there has ever been a typical Mediterranean diet, saying that "the only things that one really finds in common with the eating habits of the people of the Mediterranean nations are olive oil and hard physical work."

17   Whether the Mediterranean diet is applicable to those living anywhere, even in the Mediterranean, in the 1990s is open to question. Anthropology professor Dwight Heath of Brown University says that because of differences in **temperament** and traditions, there is a more fundamental problem in applying the diet to our times.

18   "We simply do not and cannot live in their world," says Heath, who points out that the people in the study not only ate healthy foods, but engaged in **robust** physical activity every day, took a daily siesta, sat down with their families twice daily for prolonged meals, and had strong, interlocking support systems among families, neighbors and friends.

19   Although the Mediterranean Diet may not be the cure for everything that ails us, even its most vocal opponents concur that there is a good deal of wisdom inherent in the pyramid. Nearly everybody agrees, for example, that we should eat less red meat. While Willet and several others feel that it should be forbidden completely, most take a more moderate approach and agree with food writer Paula Wolfert who says that "people like the taste of meat and once they can afford it, they simply don't want to give it up."

20   Ironically, Wolfert points out, even the people in Crete and Sicily now eat far more meat than when the original studies were carried out. In both places, meat is stuffed into every vegetable and is so much a part of every casserole of beans or rice that sometimes the vegetables or legumes become the least important ingredient in those dishes.

21   There is broad agreement on other aspects of a Western diet as well. In addition to reducing red meat consumption, the amount of saturated fats[4] we consume should also be reduced; there should be a major shift toward foods from plant sources; and that olive oil, fruits, vegetables, legumes, whole wheat and nuts are valuable sources of antioxidants, all of which prevent the buildup of fat deposits on the walls of the arteries.

22   A survey of many of those presenting papers at the conference also disclosed that nearly all agreed that even moderate amounts of exercise, if carried out regularly, together with intelligent dining patterns, can improve our health.

23   There is no question that diet and lifestyle play a vital role in the prevention of many diseases. The Mediterranean Diet may or may not point the way to good health but, as the **charismatic** Willet himself points out, "perhaps the question we should be asking ourselves is how, almost two millennia ago, the ancient Greeks managed to eat a delicious diet as healthful as any we now know in the world."

Enter your finishing time: _____ : _____ Total number of minutes spent reading: _____ Divide 619 by the number of minutes: _____ Your reading rate: _____ words per minute. Did you improve your time? If not, keep working to improve your reading speed.

---

[3]"Bias in sampling techniques" means they felt that the statistics were not designed well.

[4]Saturated fats are fats that get thick when chilled, such as butter or lard.

After You Read

Comprehension

1. What is the good news about diet, as found in two conferences?

2. What is the "Mediterranean Diet"?

3. Where did doctors in the 1950s find the lowest rates of heart disease?

4. What kinds of dessert are eaten in a Mediterranean diet?

5. What are two important parts of the Mediterranean diet?

6. How much red meat should be eaten, according to the article?

7. Why are olives and olive oil beneficial to one's health?

8. Why might small amounts of wine be healthy?

9. What are some of the arguments against the Mediterranean Diet?

10. According to Dr. Raz and Dr. Heath, what other factors should be considered besides diet?

11. How has the Mediterranean diet changed over the past few years?

12. What is your opinion of the Mediterranean Diet? Is your diet similar to it?

Vocabulary Building

The words in the following list are from the reading. Write the correct word in each blank.

arteries	coronary	longevity
charismatic	diabetes	pinnacle
cholesterol	genetics	robust
conspicuous	legumes	temperament

1. Another word for one's personality is _____.

2. Someone with a pleasing personality is _____.

3. _____ carry blood from the heart to the body.

4. Someone who suffers from _____ should not eat a lot of sugar.

5. The top of something is called its _____.

6. Beans and peanuts are types of _____.

7. If someone is in excellent health, he might be called _____.

8. The length of time one lives is called _____.

9. Too much _____ can lead to _____ disease.

10. If someone stands out in a crowd, she is _____.

11. _____ is the study of how characteristics are passed from generation to generation.

PUTTING IT ALL TOGETHER

Read More

Find an article in a newspaper, magazine, or on the Internet that talks about diet and health. Read it, then write in your *reading journal* about it. Discuss some of these ideas:

- ideas in the article that interested you

- parts that confused you

- how this story relates to your life, or to someone you know

Then, report to your class about the article you found.

Write

Choose one of these topics to write about:

1. Do you have a favorite recipe? Write it down, explaining the ingredients and how to prepare it.

2. What are the advantages and disadvantages of fast food? Write a short essay explaining your ideas.

3. In a newspaper advice column, you see the following letter:

Dear Aunt Advice:

I feel so fat! I don't know what to do. Can you give me some advice on how I can lose some weight and be healthier? Do I have to exercise? I really don't like to.

—Frustrated in Fargo

After reading this chapter, what advice would you give "Frustrated"? Work with a partner, and reply to this letter. You may give your advice orally or in a reply letter.

CHECK YOUR PROGRESS

On a scale of 1 to 5, rate how well you have mastered the goals set at the beginning of the chapter:

1 2 3 4 5   use comparisons and contrasts in reading.

1 2 3 4 5   increase your reading speed to finish work faster and increase comprehension.

1 2 3 4 5   manage your time to accomplish your assignments more effectively.

1 2 3 4 5   organize your notes for a test.

1 2 3 4 5   (your own goal)_____

1 2 3 4 5   (your own goal)_____

If you've given yourself a 3 or lower on any of these goals:

- visit the *Tapestry* web site for additional practice.

- ask your instructor for extra help.

- review the sections of the chapter that you found difficult.

- work with a partner or study group to further your progress.

Look at the photo. Then discuss these questions with your classmates:

- What does this photo show?
- What do you know about child labor?
- Should children always be prevented from working?

5

NOT CHILD'S PLAY: WORK

It is commonly accepted that most adults must work to support themselves. But what about children? In many cultures, it is common for children to contribute to their families' income by working. However, many people condemn such practices, and believe that children should be educated before going to work. This chapter looks at different concerns about child labor.

Setting Goals

In this chapter you will learn how to:

◈ distinguish between facts and opinions.

◈ read newspapers and magazines to stay informed about current issues and arguments.

◈ learn about arguments to understand the intention of a piece of writing.

◈ use flash cards to study for tests.

What other goals do you have for this chapter? Write two more in the blanks.

_____

_____

Getting Started

This chapter looks at the issue of child labor in the world. Read these titles:

- "India's Young Workers: Poverty Makes Child Labor a Way of Life," an essay by Somini Sengupta
- "Illegal Child Labor Not Just a Foreign Problem," an essay by David Foster and Farrell Kramer
- "Nike Needs To Raise Workers' Minimum Wage, Not Minimum Age," a persuasive essay by Bob Herbert

1. Based on these titles, predict the ideas that this chapter will cover. List them here.

   _____

   _____

   _____

2. What do you already know about child labor problems?

   _____

   _____

   _____

3. What countries do you think have the biggest child labor problems? Why?

   _____

   _____

   _____

4. Is child labor common in your home country? Do you think it's a problem in the United States and Canada?

   _____

   _____

   _____

5. Look ahead at the pictures and charts in this chapter. What do these tell you about the topic of the chapter?

   _____

   _____

   _____

6. What do you want to learn from this chapter? Write two questions you have about child labor.

_____

_____

_____

Getting Ready to Read

TUNING IN: "Child Labor"

© CNN

Watch the CNN video about child labor. Discuss these questions with your class:

- What problems exist with child labor?
- Who is Elizabeth Dole? What was her professional position at the time of the story?
- Why does she want to raise fines on companies who hire workers illegally?
- Why do some businesses hire workers illegally?
- Which businesses hire a lot of illegal labor?

Vocabulary Check

Which of these words do you already know? Check them. Work with a partner to find the meanings of new words. Use a dictionary, if necessary. You can add any new words you learn to your vocabulary log.

_____ advocate (noun)	_____ sludge
_____ bangles	_____ specter
_____ forage	_____ spindly
_____ languish	_____ sweatshop
_____ sanction	_____ tannery
_____ scour	_____ tariff
_____ shantytown	_____ threadbare
_____ shard	_____ tuberculosis

◆**Read**

The International Labour Organization was formed in 1919, after World War I.

Reading 1: India's Young Workers: Poverty Makes Child Labor a Way of Life

by Somini Sengupta

1 Calcutta, India—Every morning, 9-year-old Mohammed Faizullah rises with the crows and goes **foraging** in the city's trash dumps. As light creeps into the sky, his eyes **scour** the heaps of garbage, zeroing in on the recyclable treasures—a plastic jar that once held hair oil, **shards** of broken blue and yellow glass, a used battery.

2   A kilogram of plastic fetches 12 rupees—about 40 American cents—and rubber as much as five rupees a kilo. On a good day, Mohammed, a **spindly** boy bursting with energy, brings home 15 rupees—a contribution vital to sustaining his family's **threadbare** existence in a roadside **shantytown.**

3   Child labor is nothing new to India. It has long been illegal, and there have been several efforts by the government to abolish the practice. Still, an estimated 44 million Indian children work for a living—the largest labor pool of any country. In recent years, the International Labour Organization, armed with a multimillion-dollar grant from the German government, has been trying to coax kids like Mohammed out of the labor pool and into school.

4   "The whole concept that a child should support the family is a wrong concept," said M.P.[1] Joseph, who coordinates the international agency's program in India, where, he estimates, about 12 percent of all Indian children work. By comparison, one in five children in Africa work, representing 17 percent of the region's work force. The organization does not keep comparable data from the industrialized countries, although officials acknowledged that the problem of illegal child labor persists in Europe and North America as well.

5   Some children's **advocates** in India, however, argue that kids will be relieved from work only if their families can make a decent living without them.

6   "If we can raise their family's income, their children can be liberated from child labor," said Mohammed Alangir, director of Focus, an advocacy group that runs part-time schools and health clinics for child workers in Calcutta, in part with funding from the International Labour Organization.

7   "They are being humanitarian and that's all right," he said of the international agency's efforts. "Children should play, children should go to school . . . But we have to think about the social reality."

[1]M.P. means "member of Parliament," the governing body of the country.

8   The agency's campaign comes at a time when India is opening up its economy for the first time and when the **specter** of children in **sweatshops** not only can be a source of embarrassment but also can keep the country from selling its goods abroad.

9   India became the first country to sign on to the agency's International Programme[2] on the Elimination of Child Labour two and a half years ago, and the prime minister last year announced a new national effort to crack down on child labor.

10   "It is a matter the world is concerned about . . . and we are trying to show that we are also doing our best to eliminate this problem," Labor Minister P.A. Sanghma said.

11   Nonetheless, Indian government officials vehemently oppose trade **sanctions** against countries where child labor is discovered—sanctions that have been discussed in recent world trade talks. "It is a non-**tariff** barrier [to trade] that the developed countries are trying to impose," Sanghma argued. "Unfortunately, they find problems in other countries and not in their own."

12   At the center of the global debate are children like Mohammed Faizullah, who, along with his parents and brother, lives in a one-room shack, its roof kept in place by deflated old tires, in a shantytown erected under the Number 4 Bridge in central Calcutta. Here, reality has long compelled children to earn, even when parents aspire for their youngsters to be schooled.

13   "His mother and father never learned to read. That's why I want him to," said Mohammed's mother, Fatti Bibi, referring to herself and her husband. "But we have to eat."

14   Floating in a **sludge** of mud and sewage on a recent rainy day, the settlement is home to nearly 1,000 people, many of whom, like Fatti Bibi, left their village homes for a better life in the city. There is no electricity here, and an open field in full view of the street serves as their communal bathroom.

15   And nearly every child in this community works for a living.

16   Their little fingers craft glass **bangles** and matchsticks, serve tea and biscuits, weave carpets and leather wallets, pick threads of recyclable carbon and tin from used batteries. In unregulated, often dangerous industries, their eyes sometimes turn red and glassy. Many complain of not being able to see in the dark. Their hands break out in rashes. Their lungs become heavy with **tuberculosis**, say children's advocates.

17   Mohammed Salim, a 12-year-old factory worker, shows a visitor a deep, blackened hole that has drilled through his right index finger—most likely an infection from handling battery acids and

[2]"Programme" is the British spelling. The American spelling is "program."

dirt. A watery film hangs across his eyes. "When I sleep at night," he says, "I can't close my eyelids all the way."

18   Across town, in a neighborhood called Tangra, where the stench of **tanneries** and coal-burning stoves constantly hangs in the air, Salim, a 14-year-old boy who recycles battery parts, hasn't been to school in days. He has been **languishing** at home with a bleeding nose and eyes that have become puffy and watery.

19   Among kids who pick through batteries, these are common symptoms, health workers say. As they separate the threads of carbon, tin, and paper, battery acid can splash on their hands and face. Carbon can fly into their noses and mouths.

20   Salim's mother, who also recycles batteries, says she knows that her son's ailments are probably linked to his work. But her household, like the economy of the rest of this settlement, relies on children's work.

21   "What can we do?" she says. "We are poor people."

22   One way out, Alangir says, would be to offer these families loans to start small businesses—to set up a tailor shop at home, for instance, or hawk fruit at the local market. He has urged the International Labour Organization to establish loans and other financial packages to enable kids like Salim to attend school fulltime.

23   Agency officials, however, have suggested that Alangir's group seek that kind of funding elsewhere. "We don't want to give monetary incentives," said Joseph, arguing that child labor isn't driven by poverty alone but by habit as well. "A very large percentage of parents send their children to work because they can't think of anything else," he said. "We have tried to show the children and their parents that, at a small sacrifice, the child can stop working and go to school. In the long run, this sacrifice they make . . . will be offset by the long-term returns that a child who has gone to school fetches."

24   Over the next three years, agency officials say they hope to relieve 30,000 kids from the labor pool by persuading the government to enforce child labor laws more aggressively and by persuading parents to send their kids to school.

25   Surrounded by the din of children's voices reciting the Bengali alphabet, Alangir says he applauds the international attention showered on the children of his community. But, he says, neither moral outrage nor foreign funds for schools and clinics can abolish child labor unless there are some fundamental changes in the Indian economy.

26   "Child labor has been going on for a long time," he said. "We have to wean ourselves from it slowly. The issue of child labor was never on the agenda. Now it is."

After You Read

Comprehension

1. How many children in India work illegally?

2. Why is there a child labor problem in India, according to Mohammed Alangir?

3. How can child labor affect a country's economy?

4. What dangers does child labor pose to children?

5. In what ways is the International Labour Organization involved?

6. Why does Joseph not want to give monetary incentives to families to encourage their children to go to school?

7. What solutions have been suggested to the child labor problem?

LANGUAGE LEARNING STRATEGY

Learn to distinguish between facts and opinions to better understand your reading. Writers often use both facts and opinions when they are presenting their ideas. However, it is sometimes difficult to tell the difference, especially if you are unfamiliar with the subject of the reading. Learning how to tell the difference will help you to think critically about what you read.

When determining whether something is a fact or opinion, you can ask yourself these questions:

- Could I find this information in the newspaper, or in a similar publication? For example, if someone says, "Child labor is illegal in India," can you find that information somewhere? Could you say, "It is my opinion that child labor is illegal?" or is it better to say, "It is a fact that child labor is illegal"?

- Look for words such as "should," "would," and "could." These signal that the situation proposed isn't *real*, and therefore might just be an opinion or proposal. For example, "Stricter laws could end child labor" shows the speaker's belief. Since the speaker isn't talking about today's reality, we know it's likely to be an opinion.

(continued on next page)

Apply the Strategy

Review the article on child labor in India. Locate these sentences or phrases. Decide if they are fact or opinion, and list your reasons. Discuss your findings with your classmates. The first one is done for you as an example. If you think one could be both fact and opinion, explain why.

Statement		Reasoning
1. A kilogram of plastic fetches 12 rupees—about 40 American cents.	☑ Fact ☐ Opinion	**Reason:** This is verifiable information. The amount that something costs isn't an opinion.
2. Child labor…has long been illegal [in India].	☐ Fact ☐ Opinion	**Reason:**
3. An estimated 44 million Indian children work for a living.	☐ Fact ☐ Opinion	**Reason:**
4. The whole concept that a child should support the family is a wrong concept.	☐ Fact ☐ Opinion	**Reason:**
5. [Children] will be relieved from work only if their families can make a decent living without them.	☐ Fact ☐ Opinion	**Reason**
6. India became the first country to sign on to the agency's International Programme on the Elimination of Child Labour.	☐ Fact ☐ Opinion	**Reason:**
7. [Developed countries] find problems in other countries and not in their own.	☐ Fact ☐ Opinion	**Reason:**
8. One way out [of child labor problems] would be to offer… families loans to start small businesses.	☐ Fact ☐ Opinion	**Reason:**
9. Child labor isn't driven by poverty alone but by habit as well.	☐ Fact ☐ Opinion	**Reason:**
10. A very large percentage of parents send their children to work because they can't think of anything else.	☐ Fact ☐ Opinion	**Reason:**

ACADEMIC POWER STRATEGY

Read newspapers and magazines to stay informed about current issues and arguments. Many students find they don't have enough time to keep up with current events. They stop reading newspapers and magazines when they go to college because they have so much reading to do for their courses. However, reading about current events can help you in your course work.

- Many problems in courses such as history, sociology, or psychology, have direct connections to current events. Knowing what those events are will help you to put your course reading into context.

- Reading newspapers and magazines provides you with reading practice.

- Reading about current events helps you to understand how people assemble their arguments.

Apply the Strategy

Find a weekly news magazine and bring it to class. Read one of the main news articles in it. Complete the following information, and discuss the article with your class:

Title: _____

Magazine: _____

Brief Summary: _____

_____

_____

What controversies are there over this topic? _____

_____

What groups of people are involved? _____

_____

What connections do you see to any of your college courses?

_____

_____

Test-Taking Tip

Use flash cards to help you study for a test. Flash cards are useful study tools because they are easy to make and easy to carry. When you have a test, write important facts, ideas, and questions on flash cards. Whenever you have a few free minutes, test yourself on the information on your flash cards. You can also use them with a partner to test each other.

Vocabulary Building

Complete the following sentences, showing that you understand the meaning of the word in bold type.

1. Animals often **forage** for _____.
2. I needed to **scour** my book _____.
3. If something is **threadbare,** it _____.
4. A **shantytown** _____.
5. The meaning of **advocacy** is _____.
6. A **sweatshop** _____.
7. The U.S. has **sanctions** against _____
    for _____.
8. A **tariff** is _____.
9. **Tuberculosis** should be _____.

Getting Ready to Read

The next reading talks about child labor in an unexpected place: the United States. Did you know that illegal child labor is a problem in the U.S. as well as less developed countries? Discuss this with your classmates.

In March 1996, the Egyptian parliament adopted a new "comprehensive labor law" which raised the minimum age for employment from 12 to 14.

Vocabulary Check

Which of these words and phrases do you already know? Check them. Work with a partner to find the meanings of new words. You can add any new words you learn to your vocabulary log.

_____ anomaly   _____ deem

_____ carbon monoxide   _____ eradicate

_____ census   _____ laborious

_____ migrant workers   _____ sorghum

_____ onerous   _____ taint

_____ packing plant   _____ vulnerable

_____ peddle   _____ yank

Read

Reading 2: Illegal Child Labor Not Just a Foreign Problem

by David Foster and Farrell Kramer

1   From the **packing plants** of Washington to the sweatshops of New York City, poor and **vulnerable** children—especially those of **migrant workers** and illegal immigrants—are working long hours for low pay and being robbed of their childhood. A study estimates that 290,200 children were employed unlawfully in the United States last year. Among them were 59,600 children younger than 14.

2   Fifty-nine years after Congress outlawed child labor in its most **onerous** forms, underage workers still toil in fields and factories scattered throughout America. The poorest and most vulnerable among them start working before other children start kindergarten. Many earn wages below the legal minimum, often in jobs that are exhausting, even hazardous.

3   These children live in a world apart from most Americans, hidden from consumers and even the companies that buy the product of their labor. Yet those products can sometimes be as close as the local mall or the corner grocery.

4   In the past five months, the Associated Press found 165 children working illegally in 16 states, from the chili fields of New Mexico to the sweatshops of New York City.

5   They are children such as Angel Oliveras, 4, who stumbled between chili pepper plants as tall as his chin in New Mexico's fall harvest. Children such as Vielesee Cassell, 13, who spent the summer folding and bagging dresses in a Texas sweatshop. Children such as Bruce Lawrence, at 8 already a three-year veteran of Florida's bean fields.

6   The Associated Press was able to follow the work products of 50 children to more than two dozen companies, including Campbell Soup Company, Chi-Chi's Mexican restaurants, ConAgra, Costco, H.J. Heinz, Newman's Own, J.C. Penney, Pillsbury, Sears and Wal-Mart.

7   All the companies that responded condemned illegal child labor. Many launched investigations when told of suppliers that employ underage workers.

8   "If they are, that's against the law and they're gone—they don't supply to Campbell Soup Company," said spokesman Kevin Lowery.

9   Although the number of children traced to any one company was small, there are uncounted thousands of boys and girls like Angel, Vielesee, and Bruce. No one knows just how many because no one, the federal government included, has tried to count them all.

10   To make an estimate, the Associated Press had Rutgers University labor economist Douglas Kruse analyze monthly **census** surveys and other workplace and population data collected by the federal government.

11   His study estimates that 290,200 children were employed unlawfully last year. Some were older teens working a few too many hours in after-school jobs. But also among them were 59,600 children younger than 14 and 13,100 who worked in garment sweatshops, defined as factories with repeated labor violations.

Other estimates:

- Close to 4 percent of all 12- to 17-year-olds working in any given week were employed illegally.

- Employers saved $155 million in wages last year by hiring underage workers instead of legal workers.

12   Kruse's study could not account for all children who work illegally because available data are limited. For example, census-takers, like labor enforcement agents, have trouble finding the very kids who are among the most easily exploited: children of migrant workers, illegal immigrants, and the very young.

13   Even so, Labor Secretary Alexis Herman called the study more comprehensive than anything her department had produced.

14   She said the Associated Press' numbers, and the young faces behind them, highlight a home-grown version of what the Clinton administration and corporate leaders have addressed largely as a foreign problem.

15   "I don't think that we can lead from a position of integrity and be a world leader if our own domestic house is not in order," she said.

16   Jim Sinegal, president of Costco Wholesale Corporation, said his company has monitored overseas suppliers for years to avoid products made with child labor.

17   However, the company acknowledged buying cherries from a packing plant in Washington state where Flor Trujillo, 15, and six other workers younger than 16 were sickened by **carbon monoxide** last July. Children younger than 16 are prohibited by federal law from working in such plants.

18   "We obviously have to take a look a little closer to home," Sinegal said.

19   Look to a bustling street in New York City's borough of Queens, where Koon-yu Chow, 15, was found stitching dresses at a garment factory sewing machine last summer. Dresses were being made for Betsy's Things, a label sold at Sears, until state labor investigators inspected the place and Betsy's Things took its business elsewhere.

20   Walk into Grayson Sewing in Sherman, Texas. There, Vielesee was one of seven children federal investigators found folding and bagging dresses for as long as 12 hours a day. All seven were younger than 14; the youngest was 9. J.C. Penney acknowledged making two purchases of garments from Grayson, a company that investigators called a sweatshop.

21   Rise before dawn to join Angel and six other children younger than 12 in a New Mexico field.

22   "Hurry up, son," Angel's mother called. "It's time to pick."

23   The 4-year-old pushed back an adult-sized baseball cap from his eyes and turned to the work that would occupy him for the next eight hours on this October day: **yanking** chilies from the plants and dropping them with hollow thumps into his mother's bucket.

24   Follow the chilies and the trail leads to Texas, to a processor that makes Old El Paso salsa for Pillsbury. The processor also supplies a California plant operated by Cantisano Foods, which makes salsa for the Newman's Own label.

25   Told of this, actor Paul Newman, founder of the company, flew to New Mexico earlier this month to investigate. Cantisano said that, at Newman's request, it had stopped doing business with the Texas supplier.

26   If his company can't ensure that ingredients are produced without child labor, Newman said, "We'll have to eliminate the product."

27   Newman said the situation is ironic, considering that his company gave $9 million to charities this year, much of it to help children.

28   "Even though we weren't aware of these infractions, I suppose we should have been," he said.

29   A century ago, more than 2 million children labored in U.S. factories, fields, and mines. The wisdom of the day regarded them as miniature adults, each one a potential Horatio Alger[1] who could rise to riches through hard work and perseverance.

30   In the early 1900s, however, public opinion moved toward a dimmer view of child labor: Too much work, too young, robs children of an education and condemns them to a lifetime of poverty and missed opportunity.

31   In 1938, Congress declared an end to "oppressive child labor," the most onerous forms of children's work, by enacting the Fair Labor Standards Act.

32   Since its passage, child labor has declined, although it is far from **eradicated.** Kruse's study, which began with 1970s figures, shows the number of illegal child workers dropping until recently, but leveling off since 1995.

33   The 1938 law set age minimums designed to ease children into the adult world of work. Those minimums remain at the heart of federal child labor law:

- Children must wait until age 16 to work in factories or during school hours.

- Children younger than 14 are barred from most jobs, except farming.

- Children younger than 12 are banned from most farming jobs but can work on their parents' farm or on a small farm exempt from federal minimum-wage laws.

- Children younger than 18, or 16 on farms, are barred from a list of jobs **deemed** hazardous.

"Hot goods"

34   Responsibility extends beyond the child's employer. Under federal law, the **taint** of illegal child labor clings to a product from the workplace to the final packager or distributor.

35   Toss a bucket of cucumbers picked on an Ohio farm by 10-year-old Laura Mares into a truckload harvested by adults and the entire load becomes "hot goods." So do any pickles or relish made from it.

36   Even with such strong laws, America's youngest workers remain among us. Drive past the right farm at the right time of year, walk down the right street, and there they are. In New York City, for example, young teens in work boots wait on a busy Brooklyn boulevard, **peddling** their labor to construction bosses who cruise by in vans.

[1]Horatio Alger (1834-99), was an American writer of boys' stories. The heroes of his over 100 books, including *Ragged Dick* (1867), achieve success by leading model lives and struggling courageously against poverty and difficulty.

37   Despite agriculture's more relaxed labor standards, it was on farms that the Associated Press most often found illegal child labor, including the most extreme cases: the youngest workers toiling the longest hours for the least pay.

38   Reporters saw 104 children working illegally in agriculture in the past five months—nearly three times the 35 that U.S. Labor Department inspectors witnessed nationwide last year, according to the department's computer records.

39   Underage workers picked cucumbers in Michigan, green peppers in Tennessee, and apples in upstate New York. Their grape-cutting knives flashed in the sunny vineyards of California, and their head lamps bobbed in the gloomy mushroom sheds of Pennsylvania. They packed peaches into crates in Illinois and hoed **sorghum** in Lubbock, Texas.

"It's not right"

40   On a hot July day near Bowling Green, Ohio, Pasqual Mares looked sadly at his 10-year-old daughter Laura, her back bent over a row of cucumbers. In a full week of harvest work, Mares said, he and his wife and their two working children had earned just $120—far below the normal minimum wage.

41   "Someday, I want my children to be treated like human beings, not like animals," he said. "It's not right that the children work. But we have to do it."

42   In a New Mexico field, Maria Perez watched her 10-year-old son Victor pick chilies. "I like him to work in the fields with me because I want him to learn that this work is hard, hot and **laborious,**" she said. "I want him to hate this, to stay in school and to study hard so he doesn't have to do this work."

43   Victor was one of 35 children younger than 12 seen picking chilies in the fields of New Mexico and West Texas. Laura Mares was among 34 kids younger than 12 spotted in Ohio's cucumber rows.

44   In the bean fields near Homestead, Florida, the Lawrence kids—Bruce, 8, Angie, 10, and Benjamin, 11—were among eight children younger than 12 picking beans one November morning.

45   "No kids in the field—especially when we've got reporters here," a crew boss at one Homestead field yelled out. Surprised parents said it was the first they'd been told that children weren't allowed.

46   Some employers on whose property reporters saw underage workers denied breaking the law, even when presented with photographs of the activity. Others blamed the kids and their parents.

47   "We tell them that we don't want children in the fields," said Tim Reynolds, whose family runs the farm where Laura worked. "But you know, migrant laborers want their kids out there. They get more produce picked."

48   Far from being **anomalies,** those young faces are windows into a larger, seldom-seen population of child workers, say those most familiar with child labor, including migrant-education workers, union organizers, priests, and school teachers.

49   "They are in the dark alleys of the big cities," or "down a dirt road," said Linda Golodner, co-chairwoman of the Washington-based Child Labor Coalition.

 **After You Read**

Comprehension

1. How many children in the United States work illegally, according to the article?

2. How was that number calculated? Why isn't there an exact number?

3. Why do employers hire underage workers?

4. How did the actor Paul Newman react to accusations that his company used child labor?

5. When did public opinion about child labor change? Why?

6. What are "hot goods"?

7. Why does Maria Perez want her son to work in the fields?

8. What is the main point of this article?

Vocabulary Building

The following words are found in the reading. Without using a dictionary, can you tell what they mean? Look at the reading again, and try to write a definition for each word based on your understanding. Indicate the part of speech (noun, verb, adjective, etc.) it is as well.

The U.S. Department of Labor was created by Congress in 1913 "to foster, promote, and develop the welfare of working people, to improve their working conditions, and to enhance their opportunities for profitable employment."

1. packing plant (*noun*)

   _____

2. vulnerable (   )

   _____

3. onerous (   )

   _____

4. census (   )

   _____

5. yank (   )

   _____

6. anomaly (   )

   _____

7. eradicate (   )

   _____

8. deem (   )

   _____

9. peddle (   )

   _____

10. taint (   )

   _____

◆ **Getting Ready to Read**   The next essay deals with a specific case of labor problems—Nike—who manufactures shoes and clothing for sports. Discuss these questions with your classmates:

- What do you already know about Nike?

- Do you own any of their goods?

LANGUAGE LEARNING STRATEGY

Learn about arguments in order to understand the intention of a piece of writing. An argument typically has a three-part structure: background information, the concessions the writer makes to the other side, and the plea—what the writer wants the reader to do or believe. When you understand this structure, you will be better able to comprehend and analyze arguments that writers make.

Apply the Strategy

As you read the next article, locate the argument that the writer is making. In the margin, mark the following elements:

A. *Background information:* This includes facts and ideas that you need in order to understand the argument.

B. *Concession:* This is where the writer shows that he or she understands any valid points the opposing side might have.

C. *Plea:* The plea is what the writer wants you to do or believe as a result of reading the essay.

One is marked beside the text for you as an example.

Vocabulary Check

Which of these words do you already know? Check them. Work with a partner to find the meanings of new words. Use a dictionary, if necessary. You can add any new words you learn to your vocabulary log.

_____ apparel	_____ demoted	_____ smokescreen
_____ canonize	_____ merit	_____ subsistence
_____ crack down	_____ sinkholes	_____ wretched

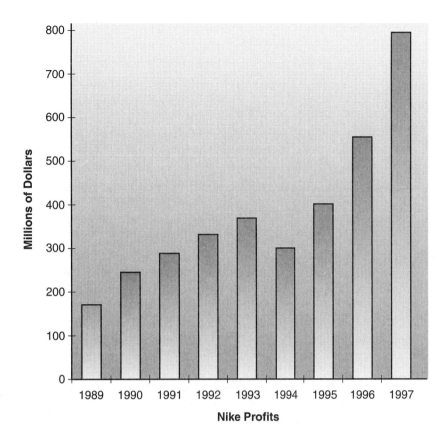

Nike Profits

Read

Reading 3: Nike Needs To Raise Workers' Minimum Wage, Not Minimum Age

by Bob Herbert

This is the 'plea'; the writer doesn't want the reader to think Nike is being generous or noble in its efforts.

1   Let's not be too quick to **canonize** Nike.

2   Philip Knight, Nike's multibillionaire chairman and chief executive, managed to generate a lot of positive press recently when he announced that independent organizations would be allowed to inspect the overseas factories that make his company's products, that he would toughen the health and safety standards in the factories, and that he would **crack down** on the use of child labor. There is both **merit** and a lot of smoke in Knight's initiative.

3   The admission into the plants of truly independent observers from local nongovernmental organizations would be a great advance. If Knight follows through in good faith on this promise, the working conditions in the factories are likely to improve, and it will be substantially more difficult for other large **apparel** companies to resist similar pledges.

4   The proposed improvements in health and safety standards, which would bring them in line with standards in the United

States, are also important. Footwear factories are equipped with heavy machinery that can cause serious injury, and much of the raw material used in the factories is toxic. Many workers at plants turning out shoes for Nike and other international companies spend their days inhaling dangerous fumes.

5   Knight's child labor initiative is another matter. It's a **smoke-screen.** Child labor has not been a big problem with Nike, and Philip Knight knows that better than anyone. But public relations is public relations. So he announces that he's not going to let the factories hire kids, and suddenly that's the headline.

6   Knight is like a three-card monte[1] player. You have to keep a close eye on him at all times. The biggest problem with Nike is that its overseas workers make **wretched,** below-**subsistence** wages. It's not the minimum age that needs raising, it's the mini-mum wage. Most of the workers in Nike factories in China and Vietnam make less than $2 a day, well below the subsistence lev-els in those countries. In Indonesia, the pay is less than $1 a day.

7   No wonder Knight has billions.

8   Human rights organizations have been saying that Nike's overseas workers need to make the equivalent of at least $3 a day to cover their basic food, shelter, and clothing needs. Medea Ben-jamin, the director of Global Exchange, a San Francisco-based group that has been monitoring Nike's practices, said, "Three dol-lars a day for Indonesia, China, and Vietnam would still be a tiny sum, but it would make a significant difference in the lives of the workers." Nike hasn't been listening.

Slave wages and more

9   Knight, in fact, has been trumpeting a recent pay increase that Nike's Indonesian workers received. It was less than $3 a month. Even with the increase, the workers are making less than $1 a day.

10   Nike blinked this month because it has been getting ham-mered in the marketplace and in the court of public opinion. As Knight put it, "The Nike product has become synonymous with slave wages, forced overtime, and arbitrary abuse."

11   You bet. And the company's current strategy is to reshape its public image while doing as little as possible for the workers. Does anyone think it was an accident that Nike set up shop in hu-man rights **sinkholes,** where labor organizing was viewed as a criminal activity and deeply impoverished workers were willing, even eager, to take their places on assembly lines and work for next to nothing?

[1]Three-card monte is a card trick that is used to cheat people out of money.

12   The abuses continue, even as Knight spends untold millions trying to show what a good guy he is. Last week I spoke by phone to a woman in Vietnam named Lap Nguyen. She was called to my attention by Thuyen Nguyen (no relation), who runs Vietnam Labor Watch, another outfit that keeps a sharp eye on Nike.

13   Nguyen worked in a factory that made Nikes. She made the mistake of speaking to American television reporters about corporal punishment and other working conditions. Despite an excellent employment history, she found herself **demoted** from team leader on an assembly line to cleaning the factory's toilets—a task, she said, that made her feel "ashamed."

14   Last month Nguyen was forced to resign.

15   Nike's still got a long way to go.

After You Read

Comprehension

1. What announcement did Mr. Knight make to the press?

2. Why does the author think Mr. Knight's idea has "both merit and a lot of smoke"?

3. What does "public relations is public relations" mean?

4. Why isn't the author impressed that Nike says it won't use child labor?

5. Why did Ms. Nguyen get in trouble at work, according to the article?

6. What is the main idea of this essay?

Vocabulary Building

This essay has several idioms or colloquial words or phrases. These kinds of words aren't usually found in dictionaries. Look back at the reading and see if you can determine what they mean. Discuss with a partner any that you can't understand. Paraphrase (put into your own words) the sentences. Pay particular attention to the words in **bold type**.

1. Let's not be too quick to **canonize** Nike.

   _____

   _____

2. Philip Knight managed to generate a lot of **positive press**.

   _____

   _____

3. He also announced he would **crack down** on child labor.

   _____

   _____

4. There is **a lot of smoke** in Knight's initiative.

   _____

   _____

5. The proposed improvements would **bring them in line** with U.S. standards.

   _____

   _____

6. Knight's child labor initiative is a **smokescreen**.

   _____

   _____

7. Knight is like a **three-card monte player**.

   _____

   _____

8. **No wonder** Knight has billions.

   _____

   _____

9. Knight has been **trumpeting** a recent pay increase in Indonesia.

   _____

   _____

10. Nike **blinked** this month because it has been **getting hammered** in **the court of public opinion**.

    _____

    _____

11. Vietnam Labor Watch is another **outfit** that keeps **a sharp eye** on Nike.

    _____

    _____

12. Nike's still got **a long way to go**.

    _____

    _____

PUTTING IT ALL TOGETHER

Read More

Find an article in a newspaper, magazine, or on the Internet that talks about child labor or other international labor practices. Read the article, then write in your *reading journal* about it. Discuss some of these ideas:

- Ideas in the article that interested you
- Parts that you disagreed with
- Parts that confused you
- How this story relates to your life, or to someone you know

Then, report to your class about the article you found.

Roleplay

You can sometimes understand another person's point of view better by roleplaying, or imagining you are that person. Here are some roleplays you might participate in.

a. A discussion between a mother whose son works in a factory to help support the family and a labor activist who believes children should not work.

b. A reporter talking to the president of a large clothing factory that is suspected of hiring children to sew buttons on jackets.

c. A child who picks vegetables with his five brothers talking to a child who is in school.

Simulation

A simulation is like a role-play, but requires more than just talking. In a simulation, you must discuss and make decisions about an issue. Carefully read the scenario for this simulation.

Participants:

Teresa M., a child-labor advocate, who opposes all types of child labor. As a child, she picked fruit and was injured badly in a fall.

Mr. R., a government labor inspector who is open-minded about solutions, but conscientious about his job, and dislikes large companies that violate labor laws.

Mr. Q., the president of a large manufacturing company, who feels he needs children in order to stay competitive in the global marketplace. He understands the needs for controls, but thinks businesses should regulate themselves.

Ms. N., the government's Secretary of Labor. She often sides with big businesses because of the taxes they provide the government.

Mr. B., the Minister of Education, who believes firmly that children should be in school and not work under any circumstances.

Situation:

There is a long history of child labor in your country, and the child labor laws are poorly written and vague. The developed world is threatening to boycott all goods made in your country, which will cause economic chaos.

You have all formed a committee to write a new law to control child labor. You must meet and draft the language of the law, which will be passed on to the president of the country to sign. The law should be fairly simple, but include information on age limits, hours, types of labor, and wages.

Write

Do you use products sold by any of the companies listed in this chapter? What is your opinion of their use of child or low-wage workers? Write a letter to the company president to tell him or her what you think. If you can find the person's name and address (check in your library or on the Internet), send your letter if you want.

CHECK YOUR PROGRESS

On a scale of 1 to 5, rate how well you have mastered the goals set at the beginning of the chapter:

1 2 3 4 5   distinguish between fact and opinion.

1 2 3 4 5   read newspapers and magazines to stay informed
                   about current issues and arguments.

1 2 3 4 5   learn about arguments to understand the intention of a piece of writing.

1 2 3 4 5   use flash cards to study for tests.

1 2 3 4 5   (your own goal) _____

1 2 3 4 5   (your own goal) _____

If you've given yourself a 3 or lower on any of these goals:

- visit the *Tapestry* web site for additional practice.
- ask your instructor for extra help.
- review the sections of the chapter that you found difficult.
- work with a partner or study group to further your progress.

L ook at the photo. Then discuss these questions with your classmates:

- What is happening in this photo?
- What wars are happening in the world right now?
- How can people live in peace?

LET THERE BE PEACE ON EARTH: PEACE & CONFLICT

6

War is something few people desire, but many people live with as part of their daily experience. Wars arise for all kinds of reasons, and with war comes the desire and struggle for peace. Every day, somewhere in the world, there is a war. At the same time, there is someone working towards peace and resolution. In this chapter, you will read about war and efforts towards peace.

Setting Goals

In this chapter you will learn how to:

◈ contribute to class discussion with more confidence.

◈ look for a writer's point of view.

◈ preview readings to prepare to read about unfamiliar topics.

◈ prepare for open book tests.

What other goals do you have for this chapter? Write two more in the blanks.

_____

_____

◆**Getting Started**

This chapter looks at peace and conflict around the world. Read these titles:

- "I Was Far from Confident," a short essay by Zenji Abe
- "The Man from Hiroshima," a short essay by Maurizio Chierici
- "Seeds of Peace," an article by John Wallach
- "Grass," a poem by Carl Sandburg

1. Based on the titles of these readings, predict the ideas that this chapter will cover. List them here.

   _____

   _____

   _____

2. What do you already know about World War II?

   _____

   _____

   _____

3. What do you already know about conflicts in the Middle East?

   _____

   _____

   _____

4. Have you heard of the poet Carl Sandburg? What American poets do you know of?

   _____

   _____

   _____

5. Look ahead at the pictures and charts in this chapter. What do these tell you about the topic of the chapter?

   _____

   _____

   _____

6. What do you want to learn from this chapter? Write two questions you have about war and peace.

_____

_____

ACADEMIC POWER STRATEGY

Learn to contribute to class discussion with more confidence to feel more comfortable in all of your classes. Many instructors expect you to participate in class discussions. Discussions help you to formulate your ideas before you write about them or take a test. Discussions also help you to think more clearly about difficult or controversial subjects. Perhaps you are already comfortable speaking in class; however, everyone can benefit from learning some new techniques for class participation.

- Be sure you understand the instructor's policies and expectations about speaking in class. For example, does it count toward your final grade? Do you need to raise your hand to be recognized? If you aren't sure about the rules, ask.

- Try to anticipate the questions before you go to class. As you do your reading, predict what questions might arise in discussion, and think about your answers.

- Think not only about answers, but also questions to contribute to the discussion. This will help keep the discussion going in class.

- Listen to what everyone has to say, not just what the teacher is asking. This will help keep the discussion interesting for everyone.

- If you are uncomfortable speaking in class, set small goals for yourself. For example, if you usually don't speak at all, promise to speak at least once in your next class.

- Remember, talking too much is a problem, too. Be sure you are allowing everyone else to speak.

Apply the Strategy

In your journal, write a goal for participating in a class you are concerned about. Follow through on your goal, then, in your journal, write how you did. Discuss your goals and problems with your classmates.

◇ Getting Ready to Read

The next two short readings concern World War II, and the Japanese-American conflict in particular. What do you know about this conflict? With a group of classmates, make a list of all the names and places associated with the Japanese-American conflict in World War II.

Try to answer the questions at the end of the readings without looking back at them.

Vocabulary Check

Which of these words and phrases do you already know? Check them. Work with a partner to find the meanings of new words. Use a dictionary, if necessary. You can add any new words or phrases you learn to your vocabulary log.

_____ aircraft carrier   _____ pinpoint

_____ dive bombers   _____ Prince of Wales

_____ naval   _____ repulse

◇ Read

Reading 1: I Was Far from Confident

by Zenji Abe[1]

1 At Pearl Harbor we achieved more than expected. Two days later, the **naval** air force sank the British battleships "**Prince of Wales**" and "**Repulse**" off Malaysia. They were said to be unsinkable, so the central command of the navy began to be overconfident. I was far from confident.

2   In May 1942 I was assigned to the **aircraft carrier** *Junyo* to train 18 bomber pilots. My mission was to attack Dutch Harbor in the Aleutian Islands at the same time as the attack on Midway[2].

3   The commander didn't know anything about planes. Since he remembered the **dive bombers' pinpoint** strikes in the Indian Ocean, he wanted to use them. But it was not the kind of battle for dive bombers to fight. I lost four of my men. When we returned to Japan, I heard that the carriers *Akagi, Soryu* and *Hiryu* had been sunk by careless mistakes at Midway. Then I realized the war was over.

[1]Mr. Abe was stationed on the flagship **Akagi** during the attack on Pearl Harbor, the site of a battle in World War II.

[2]Site of a battle in World War II. In June 1942, the Battle of Midway was considered a turning point in the conflict between the U.S. and Japan.

◆ **After You Read**

Comprehension

Answer these questions without looking back at the reading passage.

1. Where did the battle take place?
2. What was the name of the aircraft carrier the author was on?
3. What is Midway?
4. What were *Akagi, Soryu,* and *Hiryu*?
5. Why was the commander overconfident?
6. Why did the attack on Dutch Harbor fail?
7. How does the narrator feel now? Underline words or phrases in the passage tell you this.

◆ **Getting Ready to Read**

Vocabulary Check

Which of these words and phrases do you already know? Check them. Work with a partner to find the meanings of new words. Use a dictionary, if necessary. Again, add any new items you learn to your vocabulary log.

_____ span (noun)   _____ military zone   _____ mute

_____ cumulus   _____ mission   _____ stunned

◆ **Read**

Reading 2: The Man from Hiroshima[1]

by Maurizio Chierici

1   I had command of the lead plane, the *Straight Flush*[2]. I flew over Hiroshima for fifteen minutes, studying the clouds covering the target—a bridge between the **military zone** and the city. Fifteen Japanese fighters were circling beneath me, but they're not made to fly above 29,000 feet where we were to be found. I looked up: **cumulus** clouds at 10,000, 12,000 meters. The wind was blowing them towards Hiroshima.

2   Perfect weather. I could see the target clearly: the central **span** of the bridge. I laugh now when I think of the order: "I want only the central arch of the bridge, *only* that, you understand?"

[1]The man from Hiroshima is Claude Eatherly, who flew the Boeing B-29 described in this reading. His plane carried no bombs. Mr. Eatherly is the narrator of this reading.

[2]"Straight Flush" is a term referring to a hand in poker. It is the second highest hand (the highest is a royal flush) that you can get.

3   Even if I'd guessed that we were carrying something a bit special, the houses, the roads, the city still seemed very far away from our bomb. I said to myself: This morning's just a big scare for the Japanese.

4   I transmitted the coded message, but the person who aimed the bomb made an error of 3,000 feet. Towards the city, naturally. But three thousand feet one way or the other wouldn't have made much difference: that's what I thought as I watched it drop.

5   Then the explosion **stunned** me momentarily. Hiroshima disappeared under a yellow cloud. No one spoke after that. Usually when you return from a **mission** with everyone still alive, you exchange messages with each other, impressions, congratulations. This time the radios stayed silent; three planes close together and **mute**.

6   Not for fear of the enemy, but for fear of our own words. Each one of us must have asked forgiveness for the bomb. I'm not religious and I didn't know who to ask forgiveness from, but in that moment I made a promise to myself to oppose all bombs and all wars. Never again that yellow cloud...

Test-Taking Tip

Prepare for open-book tests to help you to perform better. Here are some things you can do to prepare for open-book tests:

- use sticky notes to mark pages with important information
- write summary notes in the margins or on sheets of paper inserted into the book
- organize your notes and use a highlighting pen to mark important parts
- summarize and condense your notes
- mark quotations or passages from the reading which you are likely to use
- write key definitions or information on flash cards for easy reference.

After You Read

Comprehension

1. What was the *Straight Flush*?

2. Why wasn't the writer concerned about the Japanese fighters flying beneath him?

3. What was the target of the bomb?

4. What was the error?

5. What was the author's promise?

LANGUAGE LEARNING STRATEGY

Look for a writer's point of view to make it easier to understand a text's meaning. Point of view means the particular outlook or opinions an author holds. For example, in the reading "The Man from Hiroshima," Mr. Eatherly says, "Each one of us must have asked forgiveness for the bomb." This phrase shows that Mr. Eatherly no longer supports his own actions. He does not portray the acts as brave or heroic. Point of view can be shown sometimes by small phrases or even individual words.

Apply the Strategy

Answer the following questions about the reading. These require making inferences (see page 52) in order to understand the author's point of view.

1. "I laugh now when I think of the order: 'I want only the central arch of the bridge, *only* that, you understand?'"

   Why did he laugh? _____

   _____

2. "I said to myself: This morning's just a big scare for the Japanese."

   Why wasn't it "just a big scare"? _____

   _____

3. "Usually when you return from a mission with everyone still alive, you exchange messages with each other, impressions, congratulations. This time the radios stayed silent; three planes close together and mute."

   Why didn't they exchange messages this time? _____

   _____

4. Based on your understanding of the reading, how would you characterize the author's point of view?

   _____

   _____

◆**Getting Ready to Read**   The next essay talks about an innovative approach to solving the conflicts in the Middle East. What do you already know about the conflicts there?

LANGUAGE LEARNING STRATEGY

Preview your reading to prepare yourself to read about unfamiliar topics. Reading often presents new ideas, events, and people. It is useful to preview the text to see if you can learn something about new topics before beginning to read. This will help you to understand the reading more fully, and allow you to read without interrupting your reading to look things up.

Apply the Strategy

The following reading has many names and places that might be unfamiliar to you. Preview the reading and make a list of all the names and ideas that you may not know. Then, discuss these with a classmate and look up ones you don't know. Write a brief description of who the person is or why the place is important. One has been done for you as an example.

Name or Idea	Explanation
Henry Kissinger	He was the U.S. Secretary of State (1971–76) during the Nixon and Ford presidencies. He emphasized negotiations between Arabs and Israelis.

Vocabulary Check

Which of these words and phrases do you already know? Check them. Work with a partner to find the meanings of new words. Use a dictionary, if necessary. Add any new items you learn to your vocabulary log.

_____ accusatory

_____ adversaries

_____ emotional baggage

_____ exhilarating

_____ fanatic

_____ foster

_____ harrowing

_____ improvisational

_____ incredulous

_____ let it all hang out

_____ memento

_____ mosque

_____ redouble

_____ resiliency

_____ vernacular

_____ vindicate

China has the largest military force in the world, with over 2,930,000 active troops and 1,200,000 reserve troops.

Read

Reading 3: Seeds of Peace

by John Wallach

Making Peace

1   "Before I came here, I felt like I was walking in a dark room," said fifteen-year-old Shouq Tarawneh. "I had opinions without pictures. Seeds of Peace is like a door out of the dark," explained the Jordanian student. "I've learned there are fences of superstition among all of us. We have old opinions of each other and we're here to destroy those fences. The bravery peace needs is not any less than the bravery war needs." The same theme was echoed by Laith Arafeh, a fourteen-year-old Palestinian who noted that "making peace is much harder than making war. It takes time. It takes care. It takes patience."

2   Laith and Shouq had just spent their summer living, eating, and sleeping in wooden bunks with the first Israelis that either of them had ever met. Laith was among the initial group of forty-six Arabs and Israelis who became a footnote to history on September 13, 1993, when former Prime Minister Yitzhak Rabin and Chairman Yasser Arafat signed, in their presence, the Israeli-PLO[1] Declaration of Principles, on the South Lawn of the White House. President Clinton told the distinguished audience that included Presidents George Bush and Jimmy Carter and former secretaries of State Henry Kissinger, George Shultz, and James Baker: "In this entire assembly, no one is more important than the group of Israeli and Arab children who are seated with us today."

[1]The PLO is the Palestinian Liberation Organization

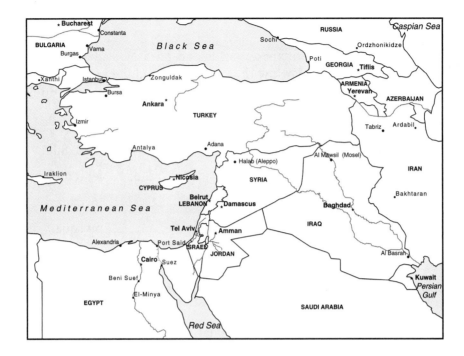

3   Indeed, these children have succeeded where their elders failed for generations before them: they spent a month making peace with each other, real peace, at a summer camp in Maine. But the task was not easy for them. It had been an emotional roller coaster that was at times painful but ultimately **exhilarating.**

The Seeds of Peace Program

4 Seeds of Peace brings thirteen- to fifteen-year-old teenagers from opposing sides of the conflict in the Middle East and the Balkans to a summer camp in Maine where they get to know one another in a relaxed and supportive environment. The aim is a simple one: to build friendships between teenagers who have been taught all their lives to hate and distrust one another, and to use these new friendships to **foster** communication, negotiation, and interchange so that they can better understand each other's perspectives on the important issues that divide them.

5   Seeds of Peace takes up where governments leave off, attempting to fulfill the hope of peace treaties that are signed but that remain essentially pieces of paper. Seeds of Peace carries out a task that governments are neither equipped for nor very interested in: transforming the hopes for peace into a new reality on the ground among populations that have been taught for decades to distrust and hate one another.

6   The program fosters education, discussion, and emotional growth through both competitive and cooperative activities and emphasizes the importance of developing non-violent mechanisms of resolving conflict. In the three years of its operation, over three hundred male and female teenagers have come from Israel, Palestine (the West Bank and Gaza), Egypt, Jordan, Morocco, and, for the first time last summer, from Serbia and Bosnia-Herzegovina. Campers are selected in a competitive process; the only prerequisite is that they must have a working knowledge of English. Initially each candidate is recommended by his or her school and then asked to write an essay on the following subject: "Why I Want to Make Peace with the Enemy." In Israel, Jordan, and Morocco, the

essays are judged by the Ministry of Education. In Egypt, Palestine, Serbia and Bosnia-Herzegovina, they are judged by a mixed panel of officials and private citizens. The final step of the selection process is a personal interview. Candidates are awarded extra points if they demonstrate skill in speaking English. Points are also awarded to children from refugee camps or other underprivileged backgrounds.

7   The program begins with a two-day orientation at The John F. Kennedy School at Harvard University. There, Dr. Leonard Hausman, the director of the Center for Social and Economic Policy in the Middle East, conducts a seminar with the youngsters. Each of them is asked to speak about the "bad things that have happened to the good people they know." One after another, the youngsters tell tales of friends or even relatives who have been killed in the Arab-Israeli or Bosnian conflict. The stories are **harrowing,** often producing tears among the participants themselves and from the invited audience. In the evening, a cruise takes the youngsters on a three-hour trip around Boston Harbor. Last summer, a folk music group entertained on board. The aim in these first forty-eight hours together is to strike a balance between the serious **emotional baggage** the youngsters share and the need to let them get acquainted and begin fostering friendships across national lines.

8   On their third day in the United States, the one hundred and thirty youngsters travel by bus to Camp Androscoggin in the tiny hamlet of Wayne, Maine. On this neutral playing field, thousands of miles from home, Laith and his Palestinian friends, who for years were accustomed to throwing rocks at their Israeli **adversaries,** are coached in the new skills of throwing an American baseball and football. The stones they used to hurl at home are used here to establish footholds in the steep climbing wall where an Israeli is taught to hold the rope for a Palestinian and vice versa. Here, on the shores of a freshwater lake, amid sun-filled days and starry nights, they play tennis and

soccer together. They paint their own peace posters. They make beaded jewelery and, of course, swim, dive, and learn how to water-ski. And as their two weeks draw to an end, all of the campers cheer wildly for their teammates on "color war," the two-day camp-wide Olympics that pits a team of Israelis, Palestinians, Jordanians, Moroccans, Egyptians, Serbians and Bosnians wearing "black" tee-shirts against a similar, mixed group of nationalities wearing "red" tee-shirts. There are no gold, silver, or bronze medals for these winners. Instead, the victorious team gets to jump in the lake first. The losers have to wait their turn.

Children Realizing Their Potential

9   Dr. Stanley Walzer, a professor emeritus of child psychiatry at Harvard University's Medical School and former chief of psychiatry at Children's Hospital in Boston, observes that it is important to select mid-adolescent teenagers to participate in this program because:

10   "The central theme of adolescence is finding an identity, a sense of self, in relation to the world. Although chronic exposure to war may constitute a significant interference with a child's social development, his or her adaptive capacities may mute the more pronounced effects of the stresses. The Seeds of Peace Program builds on the natural **resiliency** of teenagers to overcome adversity and realize their full developmental potentials."

11   Walzer, who is the resident psychiatrist at the Seeds of Peace Camp and can often be seen strolling with his arm around a homesick camper, notes that the athletic program is important because of the "central role of athletics in the adolescent development of both boys and girls." He explains:

12   "Adolescents are physically active and they frequently find themselves in school and community settings that place a high value

on athletics. Sports are a 'language' they all understand; they offer a sense of the familiar in the new and strange environment of the camping situation. Furthermore, they allow the teenagers to participate as members of a team, or individually, on the basis of interests and abilities rather than on political beliefs or ethnic backgrounds. Highly senior coaches are provided to facilitate the development of skills."

13 But these daytime activities, which also include an advanced computer program designed to teach these youngsters how to stay in touch with each other when they return home, set the stage for daily "coexistence sessions" at night. These are the meat and potatoes of the Seeds of Peace Program and are deliberately scheduled at a time when the youngsters return exhilarated from a full day of sports but are also relaxed enough to share their innermost feelings with others they previously regarded as adversaries. In their own **vernacular,** they **"let it all hang out,"** opening up to each other and confronting their own fears and prejudices for the first time in their lives. Campers are assigned to "coexistence groups," which include boys and girls from several delegations and are constant for the duration of the camp. Nine different workshops are offered, each one having a different theme, approach, and set of activities. One group may head off into the night for a hike into the woods and then be challenged to find their way back. When they return, they discuss the strategies they used: holding hands, singing, cautioning those behind them of the dangers ahead. Another group may participate in an **improvisational** theater exercise in which they are asked to resolve racist tensions that erupt between African-Americans and Caucasians in an American "inner city."

Learning the Skills of Peace

14 Conducted under the supervision of professional American, Middle Eastern and Balkan fa-

cilitators, the sessions focus on teaching the tools of making peace—listening skills, empathy, respect, effective negotiating skills, self-confidence and hope. Listening and reason replace shouting and accusation. "The growth of conflict resolution skills has been impressive in the teenagers who participated in the program for one or two years and then return as 'peer support' or as 'junior counselors,'" notes Walzer. He pointed to a group of fifteen adolescents who spontaneously started to argue under a tree near their cabin about the most explosive issue of all, Jerusalem:

15   "The interchange rapidly became loud and **accusatory,** with several children shouting at the same time. A second-year teenager who emerged as the discussion leader produced a ball-point pen from his pocket and introduced the 'rule of the pen.' Only the person holding the pen could talk and the others must listen. When another child wished to talk he or she must have the pen in hand. Although the pen received rough treatment as a result of the children's eagerness to talk, the technique worked. I might add that they arrived at an interesting agreement on how to solve the problem of Jerusalem."

16   Explains executive director Barbara Gottschalk:

17   "The goal of 'winning' is usually seen as the main objective in conflicts between people. Yet, what that means is usually subjective and short-sighted. At Seeds of Peace, we change the objective from 'winning' to 'being understood and understanding the other's point of view.' This short-term objective change makes all the difference in the way people deal with conflict. Each participant has to present his or her side in a non-threatening and forthright way so that the other side can listen non-defensively. The 'winners' are those who have made their points understandable to the other side and have been able to understand the arguments presented by the opposing side. The goal is to end with both sides be-

ing 'winners.' It is the combination of the 'team-building' athletic activities, the arts, communal living, and the coexistence programs, all conducted in an atmosphere of acceptance and understanding, that ultimately permits the children to bond and become 'seeds of peace.'"

Returning Home

18 The real test, of course, occurs when they return home to their friends and family. The ultimate success of Seeds of Peace depends on how committed these youngsters remain to an agenda that is far more difficult to implement in the slowly changing yet continuing hostile environment at home. Yeyoyoda "Yoyo" Mande'el, an Israeli, recalls that whenever Laith, his new Palestinian friend, visits his Jerusalem home, Yoyo's father says "hello" but nothing more. "My father fought in the 1948 war and in '56 and '59. He has no reason to trust them," he explains. Laith feels hurt by the silence, particularly since his own father often welcomes Yoyo to their East Jerusalem home, but says softly, "I can understand it."

19   Leen El-Wari, a Palestinian girl, says her friends simply were **incredulous** when she told them about the coexistence sessions. "They asked, 'What? You sat with Israelis? How did you talk to them and stay in the camp with them?'" Leen says she laughed and told them: "My idea before the trip was not to hate someone before knowing them. The Israelis are very nice and friendly people. It isn't difficult. Just forget for a moment that they are your enemies, and you will be friendly with them." Leen admits however that she changed few minds. "We talked and talked but I couldn't change any of their ideas. They need to meet Israeli children and talk with them to understand my point of view."

20   Ra'yd Aby Ayyash, a Jordanian boy, agrees that "telling people about the camp is not always easy. Some do not want to listen, and for others it is impossible to even talk with a Jew. But I can

understand them," he says, because "that is the way they were raised, and they did not have the chance I had. Still, many listen. Especially my good friends do. They know that judging a person based on nationality or religion is prejudice. Others do not. But I will never give up the mission that my heart found best to follow."

Pioneers for Peace

21 Perhaps the most important lessons that Seeds of Peace has taught everyone, children and adults alike, is never to underestimate what a human being, regardless of his or her age, is capable of. When the delegations arrive, I tell them on their first day in the country that each of them is like Charles Lindbergh or Amelia Earhart. They are pioneers on a course that few have been privileged to travel before: the first of their generation who have been given the opportunity to make peace with those their parents, school systems, media, and societies have condemned as "enemies." I also tell each of them that I expect that among the more than three hundred Seeds of Peace graduates are the future presidents and prime ministers of the Middle East and the Balkans.

22   So far, they have **vindicated** my dreams. In February 1994, when more than two dozen Arabs were brutally murdered by a Jewish **fanatic** while they were praying in the **mosque** at Hebron, our youngsters drafted a two-page letter to both Rabin and Arafat calling on them to **redouble** their peace efforts and never give in to terrorism of any kind. A few weeks later, a group of Israeli youngsters invited Ruba, a Palestinian girl from Jericho, to visit Ein Kerem, a suburb of Jerusalem, so she could see the house where her father was born. He had not been allowed to return since leaving in 1948 and thus had never had the opportunity to show Ruba the town and home where he spent his own childhood. The Israelis took Ruba and a few of her friends to visit Ein Kerem and amid a few tears and much laughter went back to one of the Israeli's homes for dinner.

Peace Between Peoples

23 But my favorite story is the one about another Israeli who was invited by his Palestinian friend to see Jericho, the first area in the West Bank from which Israeli troops withdrew and turned over to the Palestinian Authority. The father of the Palestinian, who was driving the two of them through Jericho, was stopped by the Palestinian police. They were suspicious that an Israeli might be up to something. Rolling down the window, the father told the policemen not to worry. "I'm just showing Jericho to my two sons," he said.

24   The Bible says that "The wolf shall live with the lamb and the leopard shall lie down with the kid, the calf and the lion and the fatling[2] together, and the little child shall lead them." Perhaps that is the most important lesson of all: after all these years, the emotional and moral power of children can still be harnessed to point the way for adults. In September 1994, Tamer Nagy, an Egyptian member of the original group of forty-six youngsters who has returned for the last two years as "peer support" and as a junior counselor, presented President Clinton with a **memento** on behalf of all the youngsters who have graduated from Seeds of Peace. He told the President eloquently, "Peace between people is more important than peace between governments." It was a line that both Clinton and Vice President Al Gore subsequently incorporated into their own speeches. On a recent trip to Jerusalem, Secretary of State Warren Christopher even took time out of his busy schedule to meet with Laith and Yoyo. When the second Israeli-Palestinian accord was signed in the East Room of the White House in September 1995, Christopher remembered that encounter. "Three months ago in Jerusalem and again three weeks ago in Washington, I met with Israeli and Arab children who spent the summer together in a program called Seeds of Peace," he said, as Arafat and Rabin were about to sign the new agreement. Behind them stood Jordan's King Hussein, Egyptian President Hosni Mubarak and President Clinton. "By developing new friendships, they are demolishing old prejudices," Christopher told them. "By reaching across communities, they are resolving a conflict that for too long has divided their peoples. It is their spirit that brings us here today. 'Their' lives. 'Their' dreams. 'Their' future. Let us not betray them."

◆After You Read

In 1981, the United Nations declared the third Tuesday of every September the "International Day of Peace."

Comprehension

1. What is "Seeds of Peace"?

2. According to Laith Arafeh, why is making peace harder than making war?

3. What happened on September 13, 1993?

4. Why are children important to the peace process, according to the article?

5. What is the goal of "Seeds of Peace"?

6. What kinds of activities are done at the camp? Why?

---

[1]A *fatling* is an archaic term for a calf, lamb, or other young animal fattened for slaughter.

7. What is the application process for "Seeds of Peace"?

8. What is a "coexistence session"? What do they do?

9. What are the "tools of making peace"?

10. How does the experience affect lives back home?

11. What does the author mean when he says, "they have vindicated my dreams"?

Vocabulary Building

Choose the correct word to fit into the blanks in the sentences below.

accusatory	improvise
adversary	incredulous
exhilarating	memento
fanatic	mosque
foster	redouble
harrowing	vindicated

1. An Islamic place of worship is called a _____.

2. Another name for a souvenir is a _____.

3. If you try extra hard, you _____ your efforts.

4. An extremely frightening situation can be called a(n) _____ experience.

5. Another name for an enemy is a(n) _____.

6. An exciting experience is also called a(n) _____ experience.

7. Someone who is overly focused on one idea is a(n) _____.

8. If you encourage someone's friendship, you _____ it.

9. If your ideas are found to be true, you can be called _____.

10. If you make things up as you go along, you _____.

11. If you blame someone for an error, you may speak in a(n) _____ tone.

12. If you can't believe what you just heard, you are _____.

TUNING IN: "King Hussein of Jordan"

© CNN

Watch the CNN video about the funeral for King Hussein of Jordan. Discuss these questions with your class:

- What world leaders attended the funeral?
- Who will be the king's successor?
- How did King Hussein die?
- How long was he king?
- What are two different things King Hussein was famous for?
- Why do you think the reporter refers to some of the world leaders as "traditional enemies" and "uneasy peacemakers"?

◆ Getting Ready to Read

The next reading is a poem. In order to understand it fully, read it more than once. You can also try reading it out loud to practice your pronunciation.

◆ Read

Reading 4: Grass

by Carl Sandburg

Pile the bodies high at Austerlitz and Waterloo.[1]
Shovel them under and let me work—
   I am the grass; I cover all.

And pile them high at Gettysburg[2]
And pile them high at Ypres and Verdun[3]
Shovel them under and let me work.
Two years, ten years, and passengers ask the conductor:
   What place is this?
   Where are we now?

   I am the grass.

   Let me work.

[1]Battle sites in Europe in a war at the beginning of the 19th century.

[2]Site of a battle during the U.S. Civil War.

[3]French battle sites during World War I.

military graveyard in France

Civil War battlefield

◆ After You Read

Over 140,000 Americans were killed in the U.S. Civil War in 1861–1865, compared to 47,000 in the Vietnam War of the 1960s and 1970s.

Comprehension

1. Who is the narrator (the speaker) of this poem?

2. Who is "them" in the phrase "pile them high"?

3. In the phrase "the passengers ask the conductor," who are the passengers?

4. Who is the conductor?

5. What is the message of this poem, in your opinion?

6. Make a list of other battlefields you could add to Sandburg's list. One has been given as an example.

   Vietnam _____ _____

   _____ _____ _____

PUTTING IT ALL TOGETHER

In this chapter, you have learned about participating in discussions, understanding authors' points of view, and previewing readings to get background information to help with your reading. In review of this chapter, choose either of the following activities.

Read More

Find an article in a newspaper, magazine, or on the Internet that talks about current peace initiatives or wars. Read the article, then write in your *reading journal* about it. Discuss some of these ideas:

- Ideas in the article that interested you
- Parts that you didn't agree with
- Parts that confused you
- How this story relates to your life, or to the life of someone you know

Then, report to your class about the article you found.

Discuss

1. Which reading from this chapter made the biggest impression on you? Why?

2. In "Seeds of Peace," one of the camp participants said it was easier to make war than to make peace. Do you agree? Why or why not?

3. In your opinion, is it possible for all wars to end? Why or why not?

Write

A. What is the Nobel Peace Prize? Who have been some of the winners? (Look up the information on the Internet or in an encyclopedia.) Who deserves to win the prize this year, in your opinion? Write a short essay defending your choice.

B. If you enjoy writing poetry, try to imitate Sandburg's style and write your own poem about war. Update the battle sites to include more recent conflicts.

Roleplay

Choose one of the following roles to play:

Zenji Abe   newspaper reporter

Claude Eatherly   John Wallach

Act out the following situations:

A. Mr. Abe and Mr. Eatherly discuss their roles in World War II and their feelings about their roles now.

B. A newspaper reporter talks to John Wallach about Seeds of Peace.

CHECK YOUR PROGRESS

On a scale of 1 to 5, rate how well you have mastered the goals set at the beginning of the chapter:

1 2 3 4 5 contribute to class discussion with more confidence.

1 2 3 4 5 look for a writer's point of view.

1 2 3 4 5 preview readings to prepare to read about unfamiliar topics.

1 2 3 4 5 prepare for open book tests.

1 2 3 4 5 (your own goal) _____

1 2 3 4 5 (your own goal) _____

If you've given yourself a 3 or lower on any of these goals:

- visit the *Tapestry* web site for additional practice.

- ask your instructor for extra help.

- review the sections of the chapter that you found difficult.

- work with a partner or study group to further your progress.

L ook at the photos. Then discuss these questions with your classmates:

- What do these photos show?
- Do you think pollution is an important issue?
- What can people do to help improve the environment?

SAVING THE PLANET: ECOLOGY

The condition of the world's environment concerns nearly everyone, although not everyone agrees about what should be done. Should people's jobs be more important than animals' habitats? How can we enjoy a modern life without harming the environment? These are the questions posed by the readings in this chapter.

Setting Goals

In this chapter you will learn how to:

- discriminate words quickly.
- learn from your mistakes on tests.
- find service learning opportunities.
- review your reading notes to increase comprehension.

What other goals do you have for this chapter? Write two more in the blanks.

_____

_____

◆Getting Started

This chapter looks at the ecology of Earth and the things that threaten its well-being. Read these titles:

- "Rainforest Remedies," an article by Christopher Hallowell
- "Our Dying Seas," a magazine story from Maclean's magazine
- "Fire and Ice," a poem by Robert Frost
- "Global Warming: Is There Still Room for Doubt?" a report by Paul Raeburn

1. Reviewing these titles, predict the ideas that this chapter will cover. List them here.

   _____

   _____

2. What do you already know about global warming?

   _____

   _____

3. What do you already know about pollution of the world's seas?

   _____

   _____

4. Have you ever heard of Robert Frost?

   _____

   _____

5. Look ahead at the pictures and charts in this chapter. What do these tell you about the topic of the chapter?

   _____

   _____

6. What do you want to learn from this chapter? Write down two questions you have about the enviornment.

   _____

   _____

Remember to take notes on the CNN video, and on all the readings you will do in this chapter.

◆**Getting Ready to Read**

Many of our drugs and medicines come from tropical rain forests, as the next reading discusses. However, many of our rain forests are threatened. How will this affect us in the future?

TUNING IN: "Medicine Hunters"

© CNN

Watch the CNN video about the "medicine hunters." Then, discuss these questions with your class:

- Who are the medicine hunters?
- What is this pharmaceutical company doing?
- Why are the rain forests so important?
- What kinds of medicines are made from rain forest resources?

LANGUAGE LEARNING STRATEGY

Learn to discriminate words quickly to improve your reading speed. As you learned on page 81, reading more quickly can help you to improve your reading comprehension. However, sometimes when you read quickly, you can misread words because some words look alike in their shapes. For example, look at the shapes of these two words:

Misreading these words in the sentence *The photo was hanging on the wall* could cause misunderstanding. You can increase your reading speed and improve your comprehension by practicing discriminating words quickly.

Apply the Strategy

The key words in bold type in the left column are taken from the next reading. Scan each line quickly, and circle each incidence of the word. (Sometimes they will occur more than once in a line.) Remember to

(continued on next page)

look at the *shapes* to help you identify the words. (Don't worry about the meanings of these words for now.) The first one is done for you as an example.

Starting time _____:_____

1. **stint**   stunt   sting   (stint)   stink
2. **poultice**   poultice   poultry   police   policy
3. **infusion**   confusion   infusion   invasion   infusion
4. **filial**   filial   final   tibia   filial
5. **girdle**   girdle   girdle   birdie   girder
6. **myriad**   myrtle   myriad   impart   mythic
7. **gaggle**   giggle   gaggle   gargle   dapple
8. **windfall**   wonderful   waterfall   windfall   whittle
9. **ferret**   turret   ferret   ferret   secret
10. **equatorial** equivalence   equatorial   equality   equator

Finishing time _____:_____

Vocabulary Check

Which of these words do you already know? Check them. Work with a partner to find the meanings of new words. Use a dictionary, if necessary. You can add any new words you learn to your vocabulary log.

_____ anesthesia   _____ ferret out   _____ myriad

_____ appendicitis   _____ filial   _____ paramount

_____ apprentice   _____ gaggle   _____ pharmacology

_____ crucible   _____ girdle   _____ pinnacle

_____ dormant   _____ hypertension   _____ poultice

_____ encroach   _____ impetus   _____ stint

_____ equatorial   _____ infusion   _____ thatched roof

Read

Reading 1: Rain Forest Remedies

by Christopher Hallowell

1 The teacher and student sit cross-legged, facing each other on the floor of the open-sided hut in Western Samoa. Behind them, the rain forest rises to the **pinnacle** of a long-**dormant** volcano. Beneath the **thatched roof,** a **gaggle** of children intently watches the proceedings. The teacher is Salome Isofea, 30, a young healer who is demonstrating her art. The man opposite her, a Westerner named Paul Alan Cox, is no ordinary student. He is a botany professor and dean at Brigham Young University in Provo, Utah, a world specialist in medicinal plants and, far from least in this exotic setting, the **paramount** chief of the nearby village of Falealupo. To people here, he is known as Nafanua, in honor of a legendary Samoan warrior goddess who once saved the village from oppression and protected its forests.

2 Salome is explaining a traditional cure for pterygium, an eye affliction common to the tropics, in which vision gradually becomes obscured as a layer of tissue **encroaches** over the cornea. The traditional cure used by healers is leaves of *Centella asiatica*, a ground-hugging vine, which Salome chews into a **poultice,** smears on a cloth and then places as a compress on the afflicted eye for three consecutive nights.

3 But before this can be done, Salome explains, there is another crucial part of the cure. Holding a coconut-shell bowl containing ashes, she flicks them in the direction of Cox, who is playing the patient. When he soberly asks why the ashes are necessary, she replies that they enhance "spiritual transmission" between healer and patient. "We Westerners have to suspend judgment at these times," says Cox. "Look at our own belief in doctors wearing white coats. In Western culture, that uniform is comparable to the 'spiritual transmission' she sees in the use of ash."

4 Moments like this are typical of Cox's experience as he scours the world's flora in search of plants that will benefit Western medicine. Cox has spent years in Samoa interviewing or **apprenticing** himself to traditional healers. He has also traveled throughout the South Pacific, as well as in Southeast Asia, South America, East Africa, and as far north as Sweden's Lapland. In Samoa alone, healers have led him and his colleagues to 74 medicinal plants that might prove useful.

5 Samoan healers concoct poultices and **infusions** from the leaves, bark, and roots of local plants, using them for conditions that range from high fever to **appendicitis.** Among them are root of 'Ago (*Curcuma longa*) for rashes, leaves of the kuava tree (*Psidium guajava*) for diarrhea, and the bark of vavae (*Ceiba pentandra*) for asthma. Virtually all the healers are women who learned their art from their mothers, who in turn learned it from their mothers. Now knowledge of the recipes and their administration, even the location of the plants in the forests, is endangered as more and more daughters forgo the long **filial** apprenticeships in favor of using Western pills and ointments.

6 For this reason, the discovery of young practicing healers like Salome delights Cox, who believes that only people like her can prevent the loss of centuries of knowledge. If he can carry Salome's knowledge to the developed world in the form of plants whose **myriad** chemical compounds might help combat incurable diseases—notably cancer, AIDS, and Alzheimer's—the **impetus** to save the Samoan rain forest, and all forests, will be that much stronger.

7 Fewer than 1% of the world's 265,000 flowering plants, most inhabiting **equatorial** regions, have been tested for their effectiveness against disease. "We haven't even scratched the surface—not even in our own backyard," says Jim Miller, director of the Missouri Botanical Garden's natural-products program. Yet nearly a quarter of prescription drugs sold in the U.S.

are based on chemicals from just 40 plant species. Examples are abundant. Codeine and morphine are derived from poppies. Vincristine and vinblastine, isolated from the rosy periwinkle, help treat cancers, including Hodgkin's disease and some leukemias. Curare, taken from several lethal Amazonian plants and often used to tip hunting arrows, is used in drugs that bolster **anesthesia.** An extract of the snakeroot plant, reserpine, traditionally employed in Asia to counteract poisonous snake bite, is the basis of a number of tranquilizers and **hypertension** drugs. Taxol, a compound in the bark of the Pacific yew, is used to treat some cases of advanced ovarian and breast cancer.

8   The drive is intensifying to collect and screen more natural products for their medicinal effects. Says Gordon Cragg, chief of the National Cancer Institute's natural-products branch: "Nature produces chemicals that no chemist would ever dream of at the laboratory bench." All this is heartening for biologists and environmentalists concerned about the dwindling of the planet's biodiversity, mostly concentrated in a wide **girdle** around the equator. Human activity, from farming to logging and road building, is chewing at this girdle, driving countless species to extinction even before they have been discovered. "I see ethnobotany—the study of the relationship between people and plants—as the key to the preservation of this vast collection of species, as well as a pathway to halting many diseases," says Cox.

9   Cox, 44, a Mormon, first came to Samoa in 1973, when he was assigned to the country for his two-year compulsory missionary service after he graduated from Brigham Young as a botany major. His father was a park ranger and his mother a wildlife and fisheries biologist; his grandfather created the Utah state park system; and his great-grandfather was a founder of Arbor Day. Cox naturally expected to end up involved in conservation, but his **stint** in Samoa surpassed all his expectations.

10   He was not only impressed by the far-reaching influence of botany that he wit-

nessed—beginning with the scene of a Samoan fisherman using a plant to poison fish in a river—but he also learned to speak and write Samoan better than many Samoans. (A difficult language, Samoan in its most elegant form requires extensive knowledge of local ritual and legend.) Cox went on to earn a doctorate in biology at Harvard, then joined Brigham Young's faculty as a botanist studying plant physiology and pollination.

11   In 1984, Cox returned to Samoa as an ethnobotanist, propelled there by personal misfortune. That year, Cox's mother had died a long and painful death from cancer. After witnessing her suffering, Cox experienced a revelation, of sorts. Well aware of the rich tradition of folk healing he had observed a decade earlier, he now hoped to find a cure for cancer. "I vowed I would do whatever I could to fight the disease that killed my mother," he writes in *Nafanua: Saving the Samoan Rain Forest,* a book that recounts his work and life in Samoa.

12   This time he brought along his wife and four young children. The family settled on the island of Savai'i in the isolated village of Falealupo, the westernmost point of Western Samoa, one of the world's poorest countries (average annual per capita income: $100). Here, far from many of the Western influences of neighboring American Samoa, Cox felt he could learn about the plants and the healers who use them before both vanished.

13   Major technological advances in screening processes have helped Cox and other ethnobotanists immensely. **Pharmacologists** must analyze between 10,000 and 17,000 chemical compounds before finding one with the potential to be tested for efficacy in humans. Until recently, animal testing and clinical trials of a single drug required an average 12 years of research and cost up to $300 million. But initial screening can now be done in a matter of days without using animals. Molecular biologists are able to isolate enzymes that can trigger human diseases, then expose those enzymes to a plant's chemical compounds. If a plant extract

blocks the action of a particular enzyme—say, one that promotes a skin inflammation—they know the plant has drug potential. By extracting specific chemicals from the leaves, roots or bark with a series of solvents and testing each sample individually, scientists can determine which of the plant's thousands of compounds actually blocks the enzyme.

14   As a result of these advances, about 100 U.S. companies are searching out plants. Drug companies and scientific institutions are collaborating on field research all over the globe, racing to study as many natural substances as possible before they, or the native people who use them, disappear. Some work with the handful of ethnobotanists like Cox to **ferret out** drug candidates based on their knowledge of indigenous peoples. Others use a broad-brush approach, mass-collecting plants whose chemical compounds might contribute to new drugs.

15   Cox is more than a healer's apprentice. He knows that if the rain forests of Samoa continue to disappear, hundreds of potential drugs hidden there may never be found. So he spends much of his time between Brigham Young semesters trying to preserve the acreage that remains. More than 80% of the lowland rain forest has already been logged. Cox's aim is to offer cash-poor Western Samoans an alternative to selling out to loggers.

16   Samoans have traditionally used the forest for hunting, collecting medicinal plants, harvesting wild fruits, and cutting trees for their dugout canoes. In this **crucible** of nature and culture, Cox believes, lies hope for conservation and the future of ethnobotany. "We can't save the forest without saving the culture," he says, "and we can't save the culture without saving the forest."

17   Cox dreams that one day soon the people of Western Samoa will see the benefit of preserving not only the rain forests surrounding their villages but also the vast cloud forests that still cloak the sides of the volcanoes that form the spine of Savai'i. Here he hopes the villagers will agree to "make the biggest national park in the whole world," before the chain saws get there, too. He wants them to become as excited about the project as he is, rather than have the impetus come from outside. Behind this goal lies a philosophy that runs through Cox's work: helping native people understand the wealth of their heritage so that they will want to preserve it rather than sell it. Since it's no less than Nafanua who is urging them on, that seems a reasonable goal.

◆ After You Read

> 8,000 years ago, there were 15 billion acres of forest on earth. Today there are fewer than 9 billion acres.

Comprehension

1. Who is Salome Isofea? What does she do?

2. Who is Paul Alan Cox? What does he do?

3. Why is Professor Cox called Nafanua?

4. What is pterygium? What is Ms. Isofea's cure for pterygium?

5. What is Cox's opinion of her healing methods?

6. How do most traditional healers learn their skills?

7. Why are traditional healing arts important?

8. Which drugs come from tropical plants?

9. What do pharmacologists do?

10. Why is the preservation of plants important, according to this article?

Vocabulary Building

Complete the following sentences, showing that you understand the words in bold type.

1. **Anesthesia** is necessary _____.

2. An **apprentice** _____.

3. When civilization **encroaches** on wildlife, _____

_____.

4. When you **ferret out** something, you _____ it.

5. If your grandmother suffers from **hypertension**, she probably takes medicine for her high _____.

6. The **impetus** for the new law was _____.

7. There was an **infusion** of _____.

Getting Ready to Read

The following reading addresses the dangers the world's oceans are facing. Although the article focuses on what Canada and its government are doing, the story is relevant to all countries. What are the current concerns about the earth's oceans? Discuss this question with your classmates.

Vocabulary Check

Which of these words and phrases do you already know? Check them. Work with a partner to find the meanings of new items. Use a dictionary, if necessary. Add any new words you learn to your vocabulary log.

_____ a no-brainer (slang)	_____ float (noun)
_____ apocalyptic	_____ marauder
_____ armageddon	_____ photosynthesis
_____ biosphere	_____ rein
_____ blip	_____ teem
_____ cutter	_____ teeter
_____ dire	_____ zooplankton

Reading Focus: Practice the Strategy

On pages 81 and 135, you learned about increasing your reading speed. For the next reading, time your speed. Keep track of your progress on the chart in the back of the book.

Read

Reading 2: Our Dying Seas

by Chris Wood

Beginning Time: _____ : _____

"We face a disaster of monumental proportions."
—Richard Cashin, Chairman,
Task Force on the Atlantic Fishery, 1993

1   The **marauder** first appeared as a bright **blip** on a radar screen aboard a Canadian Forces Aurora surveillance aircraft. The plane had been in the air for three hours, patrolling the Pacific Ocean near the international date line northwest of Hawaii. As dawn broke on the June morning, the four-engine plane dropped down for a closer look. Recalls navigator Eric Johnsrude: "We came in at about 200 feet on this guy and noticed a whole lot of **floats** in the water. The floats led us straight to a white vessel, about 150 feet long, which fit the description of a drift-net[1] boat."

2   Canadian authorities relayed that suspicion to the U.S. Coast Guard, which dispatched a **cutter** to intercept the vessel. After a two-week chase, the cutter's crew finally boarded the Cao Yu 6025, a stateless ship with a Chinese crew, south of Japan. In the hold, they found damning evidence: 110 tons of tuna and shark fins, and a drift gillnet[2] almost 20 kilometers long—an indiscriminate killer of marine life banned on the high seas under an international agreement.

3   Out of sight, and mostly out of mind, the oceans are under siege. Scientists from around the world are reporting global disturbances in the seas that threaten to bring Richard Cashin's grim warning home to every Canadian household. From the polar seas to the tropics, fish populations have collapsed or **teeter** on the brink. In a third of the Pacific, plankton that form the foundation of the marine food chain are vanishing. In every corner of the planet, increasing temperatures are obliterating some species, while driving others into unfamiliar waters. As science scrambles to make sense of uneven data, evidence points to an alarming conclusion: the sea, the cradle of life, is dying.

4   The killers are numerous. The most obvious, global overfishing, harvests 70 percent of the world's species faster than they can reproduce themselves. But the scientific community is not even sure that is the worst menace to the seas. Other major threats: human pollution, including an estimated 700 million gallons of toxic chemicals dumped into the sea each year, and global warming, widely attributed to industrial production of so-called greenhouse

[1]A drift-net is set in the water and catches fish that swim by.

[2]A gillnet is a type of net that tangles in the fish's gills, making it impossible to escape.

gases, which appears to be affecting ocean temperatures.

5   Sharply pricier seafood is only the mildest consequence; others are far more serious. In many parts of the world, fishing jobs have disappeared. On Canada's East Coast, 26,000 unemployed former fish workers drew income from the federal government's Atlantic Groundfish Strategy—15,000 from Newfoundland alone—until its $1.9 billion in funding ran out in August. Far worse, developing countries dependent on marine protein confront the risk of mass starvation. In many regions, rival national claims to the seas' diminishing harvest hold potential for armed conflict. More terrifying still is the specter of ecological **armageddon,** as the oceans lose the capacity to generate the oxygen on which life itself depends.

6   For too many species, extinction has already come. Half a century ago, 600,000 barndoor skate[3] swam North America's Atlantic seaboard. Never intentionally fished, they nonetheless frequently became ensnared in nets or on hooks. By the 1970s, scientists could find no more than 500 skate throughout its previous range. Now, they can't find any. "If bald eagles were as common as robins and then disappeared, someone would notice," says biologist Ransom Myers of Halifax's Dalhousie University. "In the ocean, no one knows. No one cares."

7   Belatedly, a handful of governments and others have begun to notice, to care and to act, moving tentatively to **rein** in the worst abuses of the seas. The patrol that spotted the Cao Yu was one of six that Canada donates each year to enforce an international ban on drift nets, blamed for killing dolphins, sharks, turtles, and seabirds, in addition to their intended catch. On September 1, the federal government designated two protected marine habitats at Race Rocks and Gabriola Passage, British Columbia—

the first in a promised chain of preserves in Canadian waters where fishing will be banned. On the same day, an international commission concluded three years of study by urging coastal nations to bury their differences and form a world authority to regulate fishing beyond the 200-mile (370-kilometer) economic zones of individual states.

8   Individuals and small groups are also taking action where they can. In Toronto, some chefs have agreed to remove swordfish from their menus out of concern for their rapidly declining numbers. In British Columbia, schoolchildren are "adopting" streams where salmon spawn, laboring to remove debris and restore the critical habitats. But such bright spots are few. "The sea is in real trouble," says Elliott Norse, founder of the Redmond, Washington-based Marine Conservation Biology Institute, "much more than we previously thought. There is major disruption even in the deep ocean." In January, 1,600 marine scientists from 65 countries joined Norse in signing a joint appeal to governments "to take decisive action to stop further irreversible damage to the sea's biological diversity and integrity."

9   Critical to the survival of marine life is plankton, the tiny plants and animals that normally **teem** near the ocean's surface, providing food for predators from salmon to seabirds. Off the U.S. west coast, scientists have detected a 70 percent drop in **zooplankton** (the animal variety) since 1950. The same decades have witnessed an even more staggering decline in the number of migratory sooty shearwaters, seabirds that dine on the tiny creatures. "It used to be the most abundant bird in the California current, by far," says biologist John McGowan of the Scripps Institution of Oceanography at San Diego. Now, 90 percent are gone.

---

[3]A skate is a large, flat fish that swims along the bottom of the ocean floor.

	Species Extinct or at Risk 1997 Mammals, land and sea		
Extinct[1]	**Extirpated[2]**	**Endangered[3]**	**Threatened[4]**
Caribou, Woodland (Queen Charlotte Islands population) (1935)	Bear, Grizzly (Prairie population)	Caribou, Peary (Banks Island and High Arctic populations)	Bison, Wood
Mink, Sea (1894)	Ferret, Black-footed	Cougar (Eastern population)	Caribou, Peary (Low Arctic population)
	Fox, Swift	Marmot (Vancouver Island)	Caribou, Woodland (Gaspé population)
	Walrus, Atlantic (Northwest Atlantic population)	Marten (Newfoundland Population)	Otter, Sea
	Whale, Gray (Atlantic population)	Whale, Beluga (St. Lawrence River, Ungava Bay and Southeast Baffin Island–Cumberland Sound populations)	Porpoise, Harbour (Northwest Atlantic population)
		Whale, Beluga (St. Lawrence River, Ungava Bay and Southeast Baffin Island–Cumberland Sound populations)	Shrew, Pacific Water
		Whale, Bowhead (Eastern and Western Arctic populations)	Townsend's Mole
		Whale, Right	Whale, Beluga (Eastern Hudson Bay Population)
		Wolverine (Eastern population)	Whale, Humpback (North Pacific population)

1. Any species that no longer exists.
2. Any species no longer existing in the wild in Canada, but occurring elsewhere.
3. Any species facing imminent extirpation or extinction.
4. Any species likely to become endangered if limiting factors are not reversed.
Source: *Environment Canada,* Canadian Wildlife Service.

10   Just how far, wide and deep the damage goes is a matter of speculation. The ocean is a big place, full of myriad creatures, whose complex relationships mankind has barely begun to identify, let alone understand. To study it, scientists must look beneath its surface, which is expensive. In developing countries, which take three-quarters of the world's fish, science of any kind is a luxury. In Canada, which exports $3 billion worth of seafood

a year, research until recently focused almost exclusively on ways to find, count and catch more fish. "In doing that," acknowledges Richard Beamish, a leading researcher at the federal government's Pacific Biological Station at Nanaimo, British Columbia, "we sacrificed the opportunity to understand the mechanisms in the ecosystem better."

11   The limits of scientific knowledge leave some of the most critical questions without any answer. One of those is whether forces big enough to wipe out seven-tenths of the zooplankton in the northeast Pacific are also affecting the ocean's capacity to generate one-half of the oxygen released into the **biosphere** each year. The crucial gas is freed from carbon dioxide as a byproduct of the same process by which plants capture carbon for growth: **photosynthesis.** "We think that photosynthesis and the carbon system have been affected in the east one-third of the Pacific," says Scripps' McGowan. "But we can't say, because we don't have the measurements."

12   Knowledgeable assessments of the sea's future often seem to have an **apocalyptic** air.

Elisabeth Mann-Borgese, Halifax-based chairwoman of the International Ocean Institute, lays most of the blame for the seas' sickness on humans—who will ultimately pay the cost. "What we are doing is killing ourselves," she says soberly. "It is the human race that will die out if we don't do something." Federal Fisheries and Oceans Minister David Anderson, under fire in the fishing community for the restrictions he has imposed on catches, also struck a **dire** note when interviewed by *Maclean's.* "We have a major crisis in the oceans," Anderson said. "If we don't start undertaking effective measures, internationally, we are dead."

Ending time: _____:_____

Beginning time minus Ending time = Number of minutes _____

Divide 1285 by (number of minutes) = _____ words per minute

How close were you to 150 words per minute?

After You Read

According to the Environmental Protection Agency of the U.S., precipitation has increased by about 1 percent over the world's continents in the last century.

Comprehension

1. What was the "marauder"? What was it doing?

2. What are the causes of vanishing marine life, according to the article?

3. What are the consequences of dying marine life?

4. What is being done to protect the seas?

5. What is plankton? Why is it important to marine life?

6. What impact has plankton death had on the east Pacific, according to biologist John McGowan?

7. What does Elisabeth Mann-Borgese believe will happen if nothing is done to protect the oceans?

Vocabulary Building

The answers to the clues for this crossword puzzle can be found in the reading. Fill in the boxes with the correct words.

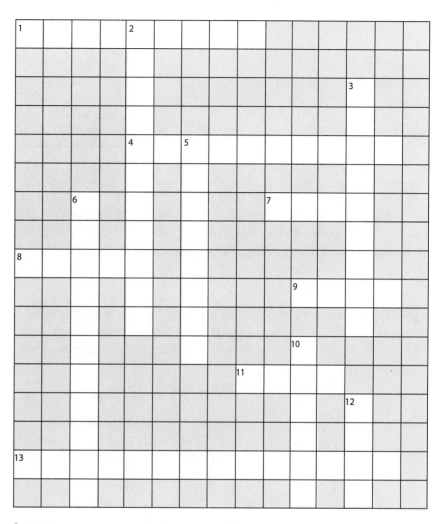

Across

1. Something that takes no thought: a ___ - _____

4. The end of the world

7. A small spot or noise; it shows up on a sonar screen

8. It keeps nets on top of the water

9. Desperate and awful

11. Abound or overflow

13. The process by which plants turn sunlight into chlorophyll

Down

2. Doomed or hopeless, according to a prophesy

3. The layer of living things on earth

5. A wandering bandit or thief

6. Extremely small living things in the ocean

10. Falter or waver; _____ on the brink

12. Control

Test-Taking Tip

Learn from your mistakes on tests:

• Look at the mistake carefully. Don't try to hide it or blame someone else for it.

• Correct it immediately. If you don't know the correct answer, find out.

• Think about *why* you made the mistake. Did you misunderstand the question? Did you not study hard enough?

• Get help from your instructor. Make an appointment to talk to your instructor about your errors.

◆ Getting Ready to Read

The next reading focuses on global warming, a topic that has been debated for many years. What does global warming mean? What causes it? Discuss these questions with your class.

Vocabulary Check

Which of these words and phrases do you already know? Check them. Work with a partner to find the meanings of new words. Use a dictionary, if necessary. Add any new words you learn to your vocabulary log.

_____ consensus	_____ endorse	_____ meteorological
_____ culprit	_____ feasible	_____ methane
_____ discern	_____ fluctuate	_____ skeptical
_____ emissions	_____ fossil fuel	_____ spur (verb)

◆ Read

Reading 3: Global Warming: Is There Still Room for Doubt?

by Paul Raeburn

1 On October 13, 1997, the CEO[1] of Exxon Corporation, Lee R. Raymond, told the 15th World Petroleum Congress in Beijing three things: First, the world isn't warming. Second, even if it were, oil and gas wouldn't be the cause. Third, no one can predict the likely future temperature rise.

2   Many others in industry and government are **skeptical** of the threats posed by global warming, and they would likely agree with Ray-

---

[1]CEO = Chief Executive Officer, or head of a corporation

The Greenhouse Effect

Some of the infrared radiation passes through the atmosphere, and some is absorbed and re-emitted in all directions by greenhouse gas molecules. The effect of this is to warm the Earth's surface and the lower atmosphere.

Some solar radiation is reflected by the Earth and the atmosphere

Solar radiation passes through the clear atmosphere

Infrared radiation is emitted from the Earth's Surface

Most radiation is absorbed by the Earth's surface and warms it

EPA *United States Environmental Protection Agency*

mond's conclusion: "Before we make choices about global climate policies, we need an open debate on the science, an analysis of the risks, and a careful consideration of the costs and benefits."

3   The call for scientific debate is 10 years too late. The costs of dealing with global warming are uncertain, but in the past decade global warming itself has become one of the most exhaustively debated subjects in science. The result is a solid **consensus** on the scientific facts. According to the consensus, Raymond's three assertions are wrong.

4   In December, 1997, 160 nations met in Kyoto, Japan, to consider a treaty designed to curb greenhouse gas emissions. On October

22, President Clinton said he would propose reducing greenhouse gas[2] emissions to 1990 levels sometime between 2008 and 2012, with further reductions after that. To meet that goal, he called for an emissions trading plan and $5 billion in tax credits and research and development to **spur** adoption of more energy-efficient technologies. Japan and Europe are pushing for even steeper cuts. The task won't be easy. U.S. emissions in 1996 were already 8.3% above 1990 levels, according to a new Energy Department report.

Assessing the Change

5 The scientific consensus on global warming comes from the Intergovernmental Panel on Climate Change (IPCC). It was established in 1988 by the World **Meteorological** Organization and the United Nations Environment Program to assess the science of climate change, determine its impacts on the environment and society, and formulate strategies to respond. More than 900 scientists from 40 countries have participated as authors or expert reviewers in the IPCC's latest report, published in 1995.

6   "It's absolutely the best assessment body we have," says Rosina Bierbaum, acting associate director for environment in the White House science adviser's office.

7   "It's a look at the state of the art—what we know about the climate system," says Gerald Meehl of the National Center for Atmospheric Research in Boulder, Colorado, a lead author for one of the report's chapters. "Literally thousands of people wind up reading these things. . . . It' s the consensus view of just about everyone who's chosen to become involved." In June, some 2,400 scientists signed a letter saying they **endorsed** the findings.

8   The basics of global warming are simple. So-called greenhouse gases—including carbon dioxide and **methane**—build up in the atmos-

phere. Carbon dioxide is the most important of the greenhouse gases generated by human activity. The gases trap the sun's heat, like a car parked in the sun with the windows closed. Couple that with a basic fact: The amount of carbon dioxide in the atmosphere has risen by 30% since pre-industrial times (about 1750). The implication is that temperatures are rising, and that's what the IPCC was charged with studying.

Human Culprits

9 In his speech, Raymond acknowledged that some measurements show warming, but added that "satellite measurements have shown no warming trend since the late 1970s. In fact," he concluded, "the earth is cooler today than it was 20 years ago." In its 1995 report, the IPCC disagreed. It said the temperature at the earth's surface, where it matters, has increased from one-half to 1 degree F since the late 19th century. The 20th century has been at least as warm as any other century since 1400 A.D., and recent years have been among the warmest on record.

10   On the causes of global warming, skeptics make the argument that most of the greenhouse effect comes from water vapor and only 4% of the carbon dioxide entering the atmosphere is due to human activity. "Leaping to cut this tiny sliver of the greenhouse pie . . . defies common sense," as Raymond put it.

11   Not so, said the IPCC—the 30% rise in atmospheric carbon dioxide during the industrial era is due to human activity and is responsible for the warming so far. In cautious language generated by extensive discussion, the IPCC produced what scientists say is the smoking gun: "The balance of evidence suggests a **discernible** human influence on global climate."

12   Last, skeptics say that predictions of future warming are notoriously inaccurate. Raymond agreed, but the IPCC doesn't. Continuing

[2]Greenhouse gases are substances that damage the ozone layer.

improvement of computer projections "has increased our confidence in their use for projection of future climate change," it said. The IPCC concluded that by 2100, temperatures could rise 2 to 6 degrees F, depending partly upon how fast carbon dioxide levels rise. That could lead to a sea-level rise of 6 to 38 inches and changes in the frequency of drought and flooding.

13   The IPCC admits there are uncertainties in the science. But that doesn't undercut the IPCC's conclusions. "This is an ongoing research problem," says Meehl.

14   Many in the business community are campaigning vigorously against limits on **fossil fuel** use, saying such curbs could stifle the economy. Environmentalists are lobbying just as hard for binding limits on greenhouse gas **emissions**. That' s a political issue, not a scientific one. And there the IPCC has no answers.

The Climate Consensus

15   These are the conclusions reached by the United Nations Intergovernmental Panel on Climate Change (IPCC), the authority on global warming:

16   *How warm will the earth get?*
The IPCC estimates that global surface temperatures could rise 2 to 6 degrees F by 2100. Temperatures have risen about half a degree to 1 degree F since the late 19th century.

17   *Are humans responsible?*
"The balance of evidence suggests a discernible human influence on global climate," according to the IPCC's 1995 report.

18   *What are global warming's consequences?*
Crop yields will **fluctuate**, improving in some areas and plummeting in others. Overall global agricultural production probably won't change. Sea level is projected to rise 6 to 38 inches. A possible increase in extreme weather could batter coastlines and cost lives. The warming would cause "significant loss of life."

19   *How costly would improvements be?*
Improvements in energy efficiency of 10% to 30% are **feasible** at little or no cost. Gains of 50% to 60% are possible in some areas. There are many options for reducing emis-sions of greenhouse gases, but some depend on lowering the cost of alternative technologies.

◈ **After You Read**

1998 was one of the warmest years of the century.

Comprehension

1. What position does Exxon's CEO take in this article?

2. What position does the article's author take?

3. What is the IPCC? Who belongs to it?

4. How do greenhouse gases affect the planet?

5. What do "skeptics" say causes global warming? Why does the IPCC disagree?

6. How much have temperatures risen since the 19th century, according to the IPCC?

7. What are the consequences of global warming?

◆ Vocabulary Building

Match the word on the left with its meaning on the right. Draw a line to its synonym.

1.	skeptical	A.	agreement
2.	consensus	B.	vary
3.	culprit	C.	distinguish
4.	emission	D.	science of weather
5.	spur	E.	possible
6.	meteorology	F.	urge
7.	endorse	G.	doubtful
8.	discern	H.	wrongdoer
9.	fluctuate	I.	approve
10.	feasible	J.	fumes

ACADEMIC POWER STRATEGY

Find service learning opportunities in order to help your community while expanding your skills. "Service learning" refers to opportunities to volunteer in your community while learning about a career or other field of interest. These are not just volunteer jobs, but positions that allow you to teach and learn. For example, a local youth center might need math tutors, or a local museum might be looking for bilingual tour guides. By teaching and participating in a new learning environment, you will improve your language and academic skills. Some colleges offer courses in service learning for college credit. Whether you participate for a class or on your own, service learning is a great way to expand your skills and knowledge.

Apply the Strategy

Find out what opportunities there are for service learning in your community. Start by finding out if your college has any service learning courses. Check the course catalogue, especially in the education department, if your school has one.

Learn about other opportunities in your community. Contact a local museum, youth organization, or similar group that offers educational courses for the public. See how you can help.

Report to your class on what you found. Prepare a handout with the names and phone numbers of organizations that offer service learning opportunities.

◆Getting Ready to Read

The last reading of this chapter is a poem by Robert Frost, an important American poet. Robert Frost (1874–1963) was a poet from the northeastern portion of the U.S. "Fire and Ice" was written in 1923, and is one of his most famous poems.

As you read the poem, reflect on the themes of the chapter.

Vocabulary Check

Which of these words do you already know? Check them. Work with a partner to find the meanings of new words. You can add any new words you learn to your vocabulary log.

_____ hold with   _____ perish   _____ suffice

◆Read

Reading 4: Fire and Ice

by Robert Frost

Some say the world will end in fire,
Some say in ice.
From what I've tasted of desire
I **hold with** those who favor fire.
But if it had to **perish** twice,
I think I know enough of hate
To say that for destruction ice
Is also great
And would **suffice**.

◆After You Read

Comprehension

1. In one or two sentences, summarize the theme of this poem.

2. What emotions are associated with fire? With ice?

3. What is the subject of this poem?

4. Do you think the world will end in ice or in fire (or neither)? Why? In modern terms, what could these images refer to? (For example, "fire" could be global warming.)

PUTTING IT ALL TOGETHER

Read More

Find an article in a newspaper, magazine, or on the Internet that talks about global warming, pollution, overfishing, or related ecological topics. Read the article, then write in your *reading journal* about it. Discuss some of these ideas:

- Ideas in the article that interested you
- Parts that you disagreed with
- Parts that confused you
- How this story relates to your life, or to someone you know

Then, report to your class about the article you found.

Discuss

Many of the topics of this chapter are controversial. What are your opinions? Help organize discussions or debates on these topics. Use your reading in this chapter, and any additional reading you have found to help support your position.

Debate 1: Global Warming
> Is global warming a threat?

Debate 2: Fishing
> Should there be laws controlling fishing? Should there be laws about which fish can be caught, in order to protect fish in danger of extinction?

Debate 3: Rain Forests
> Should Western cultures create laws that stop developing nations from logging the rain forests?

To organize your debate, at least three people should represent each side of the argument. Prepare notes in advance.

LANGUAGE LEARNING STRATEGY

Review your reading notes to increase your understanding of what you read, and to make it easier to write and talk about the issues.

Apply the Strategy

For your debate, review your reading notes. Organize them on note cards or in some other form that allows you to access them easily. Use your notes to support your position in the debates described here.

Write

Choose one of these topics to write about.

1. Do you think the ecology of the earth is improving or getting worse? Write a short essay, providing examples to support your view.

2. In your journal, write about any efforts you have taken to improve the environment (recycling, using less, and so forth). If you haven't taken any steps, explain why not, or why you don't think it's important.

CHECK YOUR PROGRESS

On a scale of 1 to 5, rate how well you have mastered the goals set at the beginning of the chapter:

1 2 3 4 5   discriminate words quickly.

1 2 3 4 5   learn from your mistakes on tests.

1 2 3 4 5   find service learning opportunities.

1 2 3 4 5   review your reading notes to increase comprehension.

1 2 3 4 5   (your own goal) _____

1 2 3 4 5   (your own goal) _____

If you've given yourself a 3 or lower on any of these goals:

- visit the *Tapestry* web site for additional practice.

- ask your instructor for extra help.

- review the sections of the chapter that you found difficult.

- work with a partner or study group to further your progress.

L ook at the photo. Then discuss these questions with your
classmates:

• Do you enjoy traveling?
• Why do you think people travel?
• Where would you like to fly to?

FLIGHTS OF FANCY: TRAVEL

In modern times, people travel more than ever. Advances in technology and lower prices have made it possible for more people to travel than ever before. This chapter explores travel and its importance to individuals and cultures. As you read, think about the importance (or lack of importance) of travel in your life.

Setting Goals

In this chapter you will learn how to:

◈ interview people in your community to expand your learning.

◈ use mnemonic devices to help you remember better.

◈ create discussion questions to focus on main ideas in readings.

◈ improve your performance on multiple-choice tests with special techniques.

What other goals do you have for this chapter? Write two more in the blanks.

_____

_____

◆Getting Started

> **Thanks to the Interstate Highway system, it is now possible to travel from coast to coast without seeing anything.**
>
> **—CHARLES KURALT, TV REPORTER**

Read these titles:

- "Selling the Sun," an article by Lars Bergan
- "Watching the Rain in Galicia," a short excerpt by Gabriel García Marquéz
- "A Small Place," a short excerpt by Jamaica Kincaid
- "Night Train to Turkistan," a chapter from a travel adventure by Stuart Stevens

1. Considering these titles, predict the ideas that this chapter will cover. List them here.

   _____

   _____

   _____

2. Have you ever heard of Gabriel García Marquéz? If so, what do you know about him?

   _____

   _____

   _____

3. Do you know where Turkistan is? If so, explain its location to classmates. If not, find it on a map and describe its location here.

   _____

   _____

   _____

4. Look ahead at the pictures and charts in this chapter. What do these tell you about the topic of the chapter?

   _____

   _____

   _____

5. What do you want to learn from this chapter? Write down two questions you have on the subject of travel.

   _____

   _____

   _____

ACADEMIC POWER STRATEGY

Apply the Strategy

Interview people in your community to expand your learning. In some of the readings in this chapter, the authors talked to others in order to get more information. This is a good way to expand your learning in all of your studies.

Find someone who has traveled extensively. It might be a teacher, a classmate, a relative, or anyone else you associate with. Write ten good questions to ask him or her about their travels. Here are some guidelines for asking good questions:

- Ask "open-ended" questions. Open-ended questions usually get more interesting answers than questions that can be answered with just "yes" or "no."

- Let the interviewee speak—even if it seems as though the person has answered your question, leave them a few seconds to think and expand on their answers.

- Tape record your interview. (Ask the interviewee first for permission.) This allows you to listen and take notes about the person's actions, not his or her words. For example, you might note that the your interviewee was smiling, or tense, or how he or she was sitting.

After your interview, listen to your tape and write up your report.

Getting Ready to Read

Most people associate travel with happy times and exciting adventures. The following reading looks at more complicated aspects of travel. Discuss these questions with your classmates.

In July 1998, U.S. tourism to Canada increased 10%.

- Is travel important to you? Why or why not?

- Is travel important to the community in which you live? Explain how.

- What effect do you think increased travel has on the world?

Vocabulary Check

Which of these words do you already know? Check them. Work with a partner to find the meanings of new words. Use a dictionary, if necessary. You can add any new words you learn to your vocabulary log.

_____ accosted	_____ hustlers	_____ patter
_____ aspires	_____ insulated	_____ revelation
_____ colonialism	_____ lackeys	_____ swindle
_____ dispossessed	_____ luring	_____ trinkets
_____ duct tape	_____ marvel	
_____ hassling	_____ middle manager	

◆ Read

Reading 1: Selling the Sun

by Lars Bergan

1 Tourism is an economic term, which gives it an air of objectivity, as if the **luring** of visitors were just another business, like auto manufacturing or banking. While any major industry affects the environment and culture of a nation, tourism is unique in its ability to change a people and its beliefs about the world.

2 In Jamaica, I have seen how the presence of the idle rich irritates the racial and social tensions of a former slave society.

3 Anyone who travels for pleasure is a tourist, from the tired **middle manger** with his American family, taking their week in the sun before returning to the station wagons and fax machines of the real world, to the European sex tourists, to weathered, wandering Australians who haven't been home for two years because they don't have money for the ticket.

4 Most Americans encounter tourism as consumers—of culture, good weather, beautiful buildings, cheap prostitutes, or any of the other things that people travel in search of. During my year as a student living in Jamaica and traveling around the Caribbean, I have seen tourism through the eyes of the people who live with it, and witnessed the corrupting effects of tourism on the cultures that depend on it for economic survival.

5 When I tell people that I was living in Jamaica on scholarship, they roll their eyes and **marvel** at my luck, because they have seen the ads for Jamaican tourism, showing empty beaches, clear blue skies, and the occasional smiling black face. I don't know how to respond, because the Jamaica that I lived in, and that only some tourists are privileged to see, is a poor, crowded, violent place where most people, from police officers to ganja (marijuana) peddlers, resent tourists for their leisure and their money—money that goes almost exclusively to a small elite of hotel owners and government officials.

6 Among the rest, who must bow, beg, sell, or steal to capture the visitors' money, tourism creates **lackeys** and **hustlers.**

7 It might be different if the tourists weren't so obvious in their appearance. Many things— dress, language, looks—can distinguish tourists from the native population. In Jamaica, it is skin color that sets the tourists apart, as 95 percent of Jamaicans are black (of African or mixed blood), and most tourists are white. A white stranger in the streets of Jamaica is assumed to be a tourist, and therefore interested in buying **trinkets,** drugs, or prostitutes.

8   Because it is impossible for white visitors to move unnoticed among the people, Jamaican tourism has moved into carefully planned ghettos of wealth. The fastest-growing sector of the tourist economy is the "all-inclusives"—hotels, generally built around a theme (family fun, swinging singles, fitness, old people), that offer one price that includes meals, drinks, tips, and transportation from the airport. Visitors to these clubs are **insulated** from the noise and heat of the Jamaican street, and the possibility of violence or **swindle.**

9   In these clubs, all of the Jamaicans are "help"—well-mannered and quiet, forbidden to receive tips. Even the phone system is different. Outside, in Jamaica, the phone company forbids the use of international phone cards to protect its long-distance monopoly. But in the resort, Americans can call home as if they were in Florida. Formal **colonialism** has almost disappeared from the Earth, but resorts feel like the newest form—the micro-colony where American money is the constitution and idleness the national purpose.

10   I spent the past six months living in St. Ann's Bay, an old fishing and agricultural town on Jamaica's North Coast. St. Ann's Bay is not a tourist town, but it lies along the main tourist road that runs from Montego Bay to Ocho Rios, a seven-mile drive to the east. I had occasion to go into Ocho Rios about once a week, taking the 50-cent minibus, crowded four to a seat.

11   Five days a week, the cruise ships would be in the harbor, and the streets would be full of pink tourists, most of them elderly, wearing shorts and looking stunned from the heat and the **hassling.** There were extra police on hand to protect the tourists, but the hustlers still owned the streets. The first few times I went into town, I made the mistake of wearing shorts (like a tourist), and heard the **patter** of all Jamaican tourist towns—"Taxi, mon?" "You like girls?" "Smoke for you!" "Come see my stand. Lovely tings." "Anyting you want, Joe." But soon I learned to dress like a "proper white man," in khakis and a clean shirt with a collar, which made me nearly invisible, free to watch the dance of idle, hungry, beautiful young men and nervous, fat, idle tourists.

12   The attitude is one of mutual incomprehension; fear on one side, envy on the other. The tourists get back on the boats believing that every Jamaican is a hustler of some kind, and the youths take the minibus back up the coast certain that every American is rich.

13   According to the Jamaican government, tourism accounts for a quarter of all jobs, and a larger percentage of the precious hard currency. Such dependence is a bitter irony in post-colonial Jamaica, granted independence from Great Britain in 1962. Like other black nations gaining their freedom in the early '60s, Jamaica was full of optimism, glad for the opportunity to stand alone and live without the domination of the industrial nations that had oppressed it for so long. Thirty-five years later, poverty and illiteracy are as common as ever, and the fate of a truly independent Jamaica could be seen in the face of a young man, 18 years old and a student in my literacy class, who wanted to learn to read so he could become a waiter or bartender in Ocho Rios. One hundred and sixty years after the abolition of slavery, he **aspires** to serve food to rich foreigners.

14   In part because of the tourism trade and the conception of Americans that it creates, Jamaica is not an easy place to be poor and white. It's hard to appreciate the plenty and chaos of the market when the din is directed at your white face and your presumably bulging pockets. I felt like a stranger for much of my time in Jamaica, because the attention was never directed at me, but at the wealthy, idle tourist I was not.

15   After a few months in the small town, my face became familiar and I was able to see, and occasionally enter, the ever-changing chaos that lives in a place where nothing runs on time. Public transportation, for example, was a **revelation.** All of the carriers are private, their

chariots ranging from 25-year old Ladas,[1] held together with **duct tape** and constant attention, to brand-new Coaster buses, air-conditioned and smooth.

16   The drivers are as various as their drives, from bragging, gold-toothed, spliff[2] smoking young men to old men from the country who never say anything. The routes went from point to point, along routes that seemed obvious after a few months but which were not marked by any signs. In the major towns there is a central bus park where the taxis and buses gather—usually just a dusty gravel lot with stands selling food, drink and cigarettes. There are several buses for the same destination, so any potential rider is **accosted** by several drivers of cars and 'ductors of buses who shout and tug to capture the fare.

17   If they don't fill up at the bus park (filling up meaning 20 people in a Toyota minivan or six in a small sedan), they drive slowly through town, calling out their destination and appealing to those walking by—"Where a' go, fadder?" "My girl, my girl." "Hey, Joe where 'a go?"

18   When I arrived in Jamaica, I envied the tourists and rich people whom I saw driving past in air-conditioned splendor, each with an entire seat to himself or herself. Not ready for the heat and discomfort of Jamaican street life, I felt strangely **dispossessed** of my identity. I never learned exactly how to act in a place where I didn't look like what I was, but I wouldn't trade my year of struggle for a year of tourism, because in some places tinted windows block out too much.

19   Tourism, perhaps, is a test of culture. For a country like Jamaica, with a history of bitterness and failure, the sight of visitors from a richer place excites envy and violence. In other Caribbean countries—Cuba comes to mind—life and music and talk keep people strong; even if they wish for dollars, they refuse to beg.

◆ After You Read

Comprehension

1. The author says that "tourism" seems like an objective idea. Do you agree that it is? Why or why not?

2. How does the author describe tourists to Jamaica?

3. How does he think tourism affects Jamaica and Jamaicans?

4. What is the difference between the tourist's Jamaica and the Jamaican's Jamaica?

5. Why do tourists stand out among Jamaicans?

6. How did the author make himself look unlike tourists?

7. How does tourism give visitors and Jamaicans the wrong impression of each other?

8. How has Jamaica changed since becoming independent?

9. Was the author rich when he lived in Jamaica? What part of the reading gives you this information?

---

[1]A Lada is a Russian car, known for being unreliable.

[2]Spliff is a slang term for marijuana.

10. How is Jamaica different from Cuba, according to the author?

11. How would you describe the author's attitude towards tourism?

12. Do you agree or disagree with him?

◇ Vocabulary Building

Choose the verb that fits in each blank in the sentences. Add the correct ending if necessary. Each verb is used once.

lure	hustle	swindle	patter	accost
marvel	insulate	hassle	aspire	

1. My family _____ to go to Mexico one day, but we need to save money.

2. Many street vendors try to _____ tourists to their stands in order to sell them trinkets.

3. If you are cheated out of some of your money, you are _____ or _____.

4. Many tour operators want to _____ their customers from the poverty of the local neighborhoods.

5. The tour group _____ at the tall buildings in New York City.

6. If someone on the street bothers you, you might feel _____ or _____.

7. The crowd was chattering, or _____.

> In 1998, visitors to Las Vegas, Nevada spent 25 billion dollars.

Test-Taking Tip

Improve your performance on multiple-choice tests by learning special techniques:

• Answer a question in your head first, before you look at the options.

• Read all the choices before selecting one.

• If you don't know an answer at all, guess intelligently:

  • If two answers are similar except for one or two words, choose one of those two.

  • If you need to complete a sentence, eliminate answers that aren't grammatical.

  • If there is no penalty for guessing, choose any answer!

LANGUAGE LEARNING STRATEGY

Use mnemonic devices to help you remember facts more clearly. A mnemonic device is any hint or clue you use to help you remember something. For example, many school children learn the names of the U.S. Great Lakes by remembering that each lake is represented by one of the first letters in the word "homes"...

Huron

Ontario

Michigan

Erie

Superior

Another example of a mnemonic device is tying a string on your bookbag as a reminder to call home. When you have information that requires memorization, mnemonic devices are a good thing to learn.

Apply the Strategy

The following list outlines things you should do if you are going to take a long trip. Try to remember one meaningful noun from each item on the list that will help you remember the entire item. You may want to underline or highlight that noun, if you think it will help.

Traveler's Checklist
Things to do

- Ask the post office to hold your mail, or ask a friend to collect it.
- Arrange for someone to take care of your pets.
- Suspend your newspaper.
- Confirm your travel times with agent.
- Put identification in and on luggage.
- Lock all windows and doors.

Things to bring

- Tickets
- Passport, visa, and health certificates
- Medical information and prescriptions
- Travelers checks, cash, or credit cards
- Lists of emergency names and addresses
- Names and addresses of places where you'll stay
- Addresses of friends and family you'll write to

Cover the list with a piece of paper. Without looking back at the list, write down everything you can remember it instructed you to do.

1. _____
2. _____
3. _____
4. _____
5. _____
6. _____
7. _____
8. _____
9. _____
10. _____
11. _____
12. _____
13. _____

How many did you remember?

◆ Getting Ready to Read

How do you feel about being a tourist? The next two short readings discuss differing attitudes towards being a tourist. As you read these articles, make notes about why each author likes or dislikes being a tourist.

> **The worst thing about being a tourist is having other tourists recognize you as a tourist.**
>
> **—RUSSELL BAKER**

Vocabulary Check

Which of these words do you already know? Check them. Work with a partner to find the meanings of new words. Use a dictionary, if necessary. You can add any new words you learn to your vocabulary log.

_____ banality	_____ mimicking	_____ superficially
_____ despise	_____ rubbish	_____ unashamedly

◆ Read

Reading 2: Watching the Rain in Galicia

by Gabriel García Marquéz

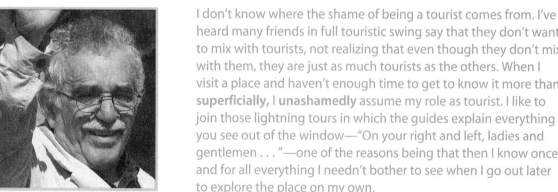

I don't know where the shame of being a tourist comes from. I've heard many friends in full touristic swing say that they don't want to mix with tourists, not realizing that even though they don't mix with them, they are just as much tourists as the others. When I visit a place and haven't enough time to get to know it more than **superficially,** I **unashamedly** assume my role as tourist. I like to join those lightning tours in which the guides explain everything you see out of the window—"On your right and left, ladies and gentlemen . . ."—one of the reasons being that then I know once and for all everything I needn't bother to see when I go out later to explore the place on my own.

Reading 3: A Small Place

by Jamaica Kincaid

An ugly thing, that is what you become when you become a tourist, an ugly, empty thing, a stupid thing, a piece of **rubbish** pausing here and there to gaze at this and taste that, and it will never occur to you that the people who inhabit the place in which you have just paused cannot stand you, that behind their closed doors they laugh at your strangeness (you do not look the way they look); the physical sight of you does not please them; you have bad manners (it is their custom to eat their food with their hands; you try eating their way, you look silly; you try eating the way you always eat, you look silly); they do not like the way you speak (you have an accent); they collapse helpless from laughter, **mimicking** the way they imagine you must look as you carry out some everyday bodily function. They do not like you. "They do not like me!" That thought never actually occurs to you. Still you feel a little uneasy. Still, you feel a little foolish. Still, you feel a little out of place. But the **banality** of your own life is very real to you; it drove you to this extreme, spending your days and your nights in the company of people who **despise** you, people you do not like really, people you would not want to have as your actual neighbor.

After You Read

Comprehension

1. Compare the points of views presented in the two readings. Write a one-sentence summary of each of the author's points of view.

García Marquéz: _____

_____

_____

Kincaid: _____

_____

_____

2. What reasons does each give for that point of view?

GARCÍA MARQUÉZ	KINCAID
_____	_____
_____	_____
_____	_____
_____	_____
_____	_____

3. Whose point of view do you agree with most? Why?

4. Write a paragraph on the same topic as you have just read. Exchange paragraphs with a classmate and read each other's opinions. Are your points of view the same, or are they greatly different?

Getting Ready to Read

The following reading is a chapter from an adventure travel book called *Night Train to Turkistan*. The author set out to follow the path of two travelers in 1935, Peter Fleming and Ella Maillart. Would you like to travel to someplace completely unknown to you? Where? Discuss this question with your class.

Vocabulary Check

Which of these words and phrases do you already know? Check them. Work with a partner to find the meanings of new words. Use a dictionary, if necessary. Add any new words you learn to your vocabulary log.

_____ ardent	_____ homogenized	_____ resolutely
_____ aridity	_____ incongruous	_____ scoff
_____ army fatigues	_____ logistics	_____ slink
_____ crew cut	_____ noncommittal	_____ stave off
_____ dispelled	_____ outposts	_____ steppes
_____ gawky	_____ rarefied	_____ stoic
_____ gubernatorial	_____ reckon	_____ unrepentant
_____ hailing	_____ reclamation	_____ wacky

TUNING IN: "Exotic Travel"

Watch the CNN video about exotic travel. Discuss these questions with your class:

- What kind of travel does this story talk about?
- What kind of people go on these kinds of vacations?
- What locations are popular?
- Which of the destinations mentioned would you enjoy visiting?

© CNN

Read

Reading 4: Night Train to Turkistan

by Stuart Stevens

1 I grew up in a family whose concept of an adventure was not confirming hotel reservations. In writing. Preferably twice.

2   My mother loved the *idea* of traveling as much as she disliked the reality of where marriage had brought her—Jackson, Mississippi.

The latter seemed to propel the former, and our house was always filled with brochures, magazines, and newsletters **hailing** the delights of exotic places.

3   Fortunately she came to realize fairly early that reading about horrible places like Peru

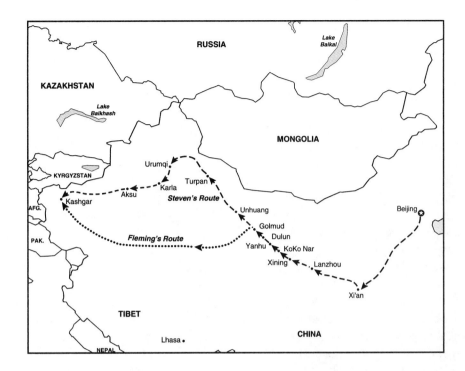

was much more fun than actually going there. After one exploration to a remote fishing camp in the then-wilds of Florida, my father announced that as far as these beautiful, un-spoiled places were concerned, he'd just as soon go back when they spoiled them a little more. This excellent advice was taken to heart, and our family safaris were henceforth restricted to **outposts** such as Sea Island, Georgia, and Grand Hotel, in Point Clear, Alabama.

4   It was at such places, usually hiding out from a **gawky** teenager with the title "activity director," that I developed a love for adventure-travel writing. And while the appeal of some ventures faded—I no longer wanted to get a bowl haircut and set out around the world on a tramp steamer[1] as Richard Halliburton had done in *The Royal Road to Romance*—thoughts of *News From Tartary* continued to **slink** around my brain, seductive and **unrepentant.**

5   The Communists had clamped the door on western China in 1949, and only in the last year or so had it become possible to enter that huge region. It was a part of the globe so remote

from Beijng that it had no business being called China. Chinese Turkistan—or Tartary—was what it had been known as for centuries, and it was hard to imagine how even the most **ardent** Communist conformity could have **homogenized** this vast and fierce territory. Though the Han Chinese—the people with the round faces and narrow eyelids that most of us think of as "true" Chinese—constitute over ninety-eight percent of China's total population, out west they are still a minority. (A situation, I'd learn, they are hard at work to change.) Chinese Turkistan had always been the land of Uighur, Kazakh, Mongol, and Hui tribesmen, some of the earth's great nomads and fighters.

6   Turkistan is a wild, contradictory territory containing the earth's highest point—Qomo-langina, or Mount Everest—and the second lowest point on dry land—the Turfan Depression, 154 meters below sea level. Jammed in between two vast mountain ranges, there is the Takla Makan desert (a name roughly translated as "you go in but do not return"), **incongruous**

---

[1]A tramp steamer is a type of freighter on which one could travel cheaply. It offered no luxuries.

swamps, and miles of high, grass-covered **steppes** that roll monotonously toward the horizon—or so I had heard.

7   In 1936, Peter Fleming said Turkistan was an area about which little more is known than Darkest Africa. Now all that was changing; but it was still, I **reckoned,** a place worth seeing, and I wanted to get there before Malcolm Forbes[2] arrived with his motorcycles, TV crews, and French chefs.

8   When I called Ella Maillart, still very much alive in Geneva, to tell her of my plans to travel in her footsteps, she **scoffed.** "You must be a very foolish and very young boy."

9   "Why?" I asked. "Everything is modern and terrible now."

10   I thought about this as we gathered our bags to leave the glass and steel Sheraton. There was a slight military feeling to our preparations. David and I wore green wool **army fatigues**; he had a couple of water bottles hanging from his belt and carried a duffel bag. Even without the pants and gear, David looked like he should belong to some elite special forces unit. His hair was about a week beyond a **crew cut,** and he had on a Marine Corps Marathon T-shirt under his jacket. He was in intimidatingly good shape; marathons and triathlons were his idea of relaxation. Before taking off from Kennedy[3] he had announced in the most genuinely off-hand manner that he planned to do 1,000 push-ups on the plane just to **stave off** restlessness.

11   I'd met David ten years before when we both worked for the same **gubernatorial** candidate in Mississippi. We lost. David was quiet and very smart, with a **stoic** sort of love for the physical punishment of eighteen-hour campaign days in Mississippi's 100-degree heat.

12   In 1984, when I had embarked on a crazy project to ski a record number of international, long-distance races, David volunteered to come with me as coach and **logistics** chief. He had to cancel at the last minute but promised, "The next weird thing you do, I'm coming. No matter what."

13   China was the next weird thing. It was just going to be the three of us—David, Mark, and I—until a few weeks before we planned to leave I got a call from a friend in Washington.

14   "I've got a **wacky** question for you."

15   "Um?"

16   "What if Fran wanted to go to China with you?"

17   He was right. It was a wacky question. Fran was Fran Trafton, a young woman who worked for him. I'd only met her once but remembered that she was tall and thin and that everyone in Washington seemed to think she was beautiful.

18   "I think she's tired of me," my friend told me when I asked why Fran wanted to go. And when I asked him how she might handle the difficulties of the journey, he said very reassuringly, "She's from Maine."

19   "Maine," I said.

20   "That means she's used to cold weather. China is cold, right?"

21   "Yes, it is," I answered, still **resolutely** unconvinced.

22   "And she's a great rower. A national champion in college."

23   This had a certain appeal. Ella Maillart was on the Swiss national sailing team. Fran was a champion rower. We were traveling through a massive desert. It made a certain kind of sense that she should come.

24   Before I invited her, I called David for his opinion.

25   He was **noncommittal** until he heard about her athletic interests.

26   "Maybe we could train together if she went," he suggested.

---

[2]Malcolm Forbes is a very wealthy man known to enjoy adventure travel, usually by motorcycle.

[3]Kennedy refers to Kennedy Airport in New York.

27　"I'm sure she'd enjoy it."

28　"I tell you what, ask her if she wants to train together and if she says yes, let's bring her."

29　I didn't do this. Instead, I called my friend and told him she could come.

30　"So what do you think about going to China?" I asked Fran when she phoned me later.

31　"Cool. Very cool," she replied. Oh, God, I thought, what have I done?

32　But my panicked vision of touring China with a Valley Girl[4] was quickly **dispelled** our first days in Beijing. And while Fran's rowing skills had yet to be utilized, her background of cold weather had proved imperative. China was the coldest place I'd ever been.

33　The Polar Continental air mass, originating in Siberia or Mongolia, dominates a large part of China during the winter. . . . The Siberian air mass is stable and extremely cold and dry. . . . Wind velocities in the win-ter monsoon, which prevails from November to March, are rather high . . . the cold is often unbearable.

34　Before leaving America, I'd read all this cheery stuff in a book called *China: Essays on Geography*. But somehow it hadn't made much of an impression during a New York summer.

35　Standing in front of the Great Wall Sheraton at dusk, eyes tearing from the wind and cold, it became a more personal matter. My God, I thought, if Beijing is like this, what would it be out west?

36　A large part of the Quinhai[Qinghai]-Tibet Plateau itself consists of cold deserts. . . . Because of the severe cold and **aridity**, **reclamation** of the land is seriously handi-capped. . . . Furthermore, as the air is **rarefied**, human activities are greatly hindered.

37　The Qinghai-Tibet Plateau was where we were headed.

◆ **After You Read**　　**Comprehension**

1. How did the author develop his love of adventure-travel writing?

2. What book influenced the author to travel to China?

3. Why did the author think that western China "had no business being called China"?

4. What is the former name of Chinese Turkistan?

5. Who are the Han Chinese?

6. Who are the indigenous inhabitants of western China?

7. What famous mountain is found in Turkistan?

8. Who is Ella Maillart? Why did she think the author's trip was foolish?

9. What kind of person is David?

10. What does the author think western China will be like?

[4]A Valley Girl refers to a girl or woman from the San Fernando Valley in Los Angeles. The stereotype of a Valley Girl is someone who enjoys shopping and is superficial.

Analysis

1. Why does the author describe the type of family he grew up in?

2. Why do you think the author was uncertain about taking Fran with them on the trip?

3. When the author refers to Peru as "a horrible place," whose opinion do you think he is reporting?

4. In the second paragraph, the author says, "My mother loved the *idea* of traveling as much as she disliked the reality of where marriage had brought her—Jackson, Mississippi. The latter seemed to propel the former. . . ." What does this mean?

◆ Vocabulary Building

The words in the column numbered 1–10 below are found in the preceding reading. Identify a synonym and an antonym for each word from the list below. The first one is done for you. Cross them off as you work.

clumsy	~~eager~~	logical	sensible
compliment	excitable	neutral	serious
crazy	graceful	purposefully	sorry
devoted	inconsistent	remorseless	weakly
dryness	~~indifferent~~	ridicule	wetness

	SYNONYM	ANTONYM
1. ardent	*eager*	*indifferent*
2. aridity		
3. gawky		
4. incongruous		
5. noncommittal		
6. resolutely		
7. scoff		
8. stoic		
9. unrepentant		
10. wacky		

PUTTING IT ALL TOGETHER

Read More

Where would you like to travel to? Do some research using newspapers, magazines, or the Internet. Find as much information as you can about the location you are interested in. Prepare a report to give in front of your class. Include the following information, as well as other information you think is interesting:

- Why you are interested in your chosen location
- Where it is located
- What the climate is like there
- What natural wonders are found there (such as mountains, rain forests, etc.)
- What historical attractions are there
- The population size and composition
- The language(s) spoken there

Discuss

LANGUAGE LEARNING STRATEGY

Create discussion questions to work on with your classmates to focus on the main ideas of your reading. When you formulate good discussion questions, you learn as much as you do when you just answer the questions in your book. Writing questions is a good way to prepare yourself to study for tests, or to talk through your understanding of a subject.

Apply the Strategy

Review your notes for the entire chapter. Write five good discussion questions to discuss with your classmates. Your questions should focus on the *ideas* presented in this chapter, not just the facts.

(continued on next page)

1. _____
   _____
2. _____
   _____
3. _____
   _____
4. _____
   _____
5. _____
   _____

Write

Choose one of these topics to write about.

1. Is tourism good for an area, or detrimental? Write a short essay expressing your opinion. Give concrete examples to support your opinion.

2. With a partner, prepare a tourist brochure for the town in which you are living. What should tourists visit? What attractions are there to see?

CHECK YOUR PROGRESS

On a scale of 1 to 5, rate how well you have mastered the goals set at the beginning of the chapter:

1 2 3 4 5   interview people in the community to expand your learning.

1 2 3 4 5   use mnemonic devices to help you remember better.

1 2 3 4 5   create discussion questions to focus on main ideas in readings.

1 2 3 4 5   improve your performance on multiple-choice tests with special techniques.

1 2 3 4 5   (your own goal) _____

1 2 3 4 5   (your own goal) _____

If you've given yourself a 3 or lower on any of these goals:

- visit the *Tapestry* web site for additional practice.
- ask your instructor for extra help.
- review the sections of the chapter that you found difficult.
- work with a partner or study group to further your progress.

L ook at the photo. Then discuss these questions with your classmates:

- Where was this photo taken?
- Are bicycles a popular form of transportation where you live?
- What do you consider "alternative" forms of transportation?

GOING PLACES: ALTERNATIVE TRANSPORTATION

How do you get where you need to go? Do you take public transportation, ride a bike, walk, or use a car? Cars are convenient, but much of the world uses other forms of transportation. This chapter looks at some alternative transportation options.

Setting Goals

In this chapter you will learn how to:

◈ find ways to overcome procrastination.

◈ use mapping to help you review a text.

◈ use context to decode unfamiliar terms.

◈ use pictures to help you to understand descriptions you read.

◈ do well on take-home tests.

What other goals do you have for this chapter? Write two more in the blanks.

_____

_____

◆ Getting Started

This chapter looks at changes in transportation around the world. Read these titles:

- "Tide of Traffic Turns Against the Sea of Bicycles," a *New York Times* article
- "Let Them Ride Bikes," a report by Jason Beaubien
- "Microcars Get Big," an article by Edward M. Gomez
- "Vehicles of the Future," an article from *Business Wire*

1. Predict the ideas that this chapter will cover. List them here.

   _____

   _____

   _____

2. What do you already know about bicycles in China?

   _____

   _____

   _____

3. What do you think the car of the future will be like?

   _____

   _____

   _____

4. Look ahead at the pictures and charts in this chapter. What do these tell you about the topic of the chapter?

   _____

   _____

   _____

5. What do you want to learn from this chapter? Write down two questions you have about alternative transportation.

   _____

   _____

   _____

ACADEMIC POWER STRATEGY

Apply the Strategy

Find ways to overcome procrastination so that you will get more work done. Does everyone procrastinate? Probably. Students often have so many tasks to complete, it's easy to become overwhelmed and put off what needs to be done. However, it is possible to overcome procrastination.

The next time you find yourself procrastinating, try these five ideas:

1. Break it down: If you have a large project to do, break it into a series of small steps that can be done in 20 minutes or less. If you have a long reading assignment, read it in 2-3 page increments. If you have a paper to write, list the steps you need to do to complete it, such as write the thesis statement, or organize your bibliography, and do only those tasks.

2. Do it now: As soon as you find yourself procrastinating, stop whatever you're doing and jump back into your task.

3. Make it public: Tell your friends and family what you intend to do—read the fourth chapter, finish studying for your chemistry exam, whatever you need to do. When you tell others, you make a commitment to them and to yourself. They may also have additional helpful suggestions for you.

4. Prioritize: Look at your to-do list and evaluate the items there. For those that are really important, move them to the top of your list, and do them immediately. However, if you have tasks that you keep putting off, perhaps you don't really need to do everything you had planned. If you really aren't going to do something, stop telling yourself that you will someday. Cross it off your list—then you're not procrastinating!

5. Reward yourself: Find a unique and meaningful way to reward yourself. Buy yourself a new CD, or go out to a movie. When you earn a reward, you will feel good twice: once for completing your task, and once for getting a reward.

◆Getting Ready to Read

© CNN

> Only 2 percent of road accidents involve bicyclists. Among those killed, the most serious injuries are head injuries. It's important for bicyclists to wear helmets.

The city of Beijing, China, has long been known for its thousands of bicycles and bicyclists. Watch the CNN video before you read.

TUNING IN: "The Beijing Bicycle Ban"

Watch the CNN video about the Chinese ban on bicycles. Discuss these questions with your class:

- Where have bicycles been banned?
- Why were they banned?
- What reaction do citizens have to the ban?
- What is your opinion of the bicycle ban?

Vocabulary Check

Which of these words do you already know? Check them. Work with a partner to find the meanings of new words. Add any new words you learn to your Vocabulary Log.

_____ a.k.a.	_____ gridlock	_____ nondescript
_____ arcane	_____ guzzle	_____ novocaine
_____ corral (verb)	_____ hapless	_____ opine
_____ fanfare	_____ mar	_____ propel

◆Read

Reading 1: Tide of Traffic Turns Against the Sea of Bicycles

by Elisabeth Rosenthal

1   BEIJING—Every day this city's wide boulevards are **marred** by a million ugly battles between "gas vehicles," as cars are called in Chinese, and "self-**propelled** vehicles"—**a.k.a.** bicycles.

2   Although sturdy bicycles remain the primary transportation for the vast majority of Beijingers, their powerful gas-**guzzling** cousins have been multiplying rapidly, literally edging cyclists off the road.

3   The thousands of cyclists who once dominated the streets have long since been **corralled** into bike lanes, where they move like slow-flowing rivers beside every road.

4   But even these reserved lanes are not sacred anymore, their flow constantly interrupted by impatient drivers darting in to avoid the city's endless traffic jams, scattering cyclists to and fro. At traffic circles and when crossing streets, the once reigning cyclists **haplessly** pick their way across four lanes of buses and cars.

5   Still, it seemed jarring last week when the inevitable occurred: To improve traffic flow, the Beijing city government for the first time declared a street to be a "no-bike" zone, claiming its bike lanes for cars.

6   With little **fanfare,** the police planted signs at either end of a short but notoriously **gridlocked** street called Xisidong Avenue, bearing a black bicycle in a red circle slashed out by a red diagonal line. They put up chalkboards explaining the ban.

7   And the **nondescript** four-lane road—home to restaurants, small stores and (perhaps significantly) the local traffic police—took on historic significance: the site where China cast its vote with a motorized future, and cast off the vehicle of the masses. More streets are to follow.

8   "I hadn't heard about it until now, and it's a pain for me," Gao Xiaohui, 21, said as he pushed his only vehicle, a silver mountain bike, along the sidewalk toward a movie theater, days after the ban. "But traffic was really bad here before—there are so many cars—I guess it had to happen."

9   Of course, in a city of more than 13 million people, where bicycles outnumber the 1.2 million cars by well over 5-to-1, and on a street where 6,000 bikes used to pass each hour at peak times, the will of the people is not easily overcome. And, late last week, it took a small army of police and government volunteers to enforce the new rules, playing cat-and-mouse with the steady trickle of bicyclists who sneaked in.

10   At each end of the street, a government worker with an armband and loudspeaker implored bike riders to get off and walk, or take alternate routes. A uniformed policemen stood 15 yards back, intercepting those who pedaled through and insisting they dismount.

11   Thus caught, a number of cyclists like Ren Bo, a middle-aged lab technician, obligingly pushed their bikes a few yards, looked over a shoulder, and hopped back on—only to be intercepted by the next volunteer some 50 yards down the street.

12   "It's very inconvenient for me—I'm in pain and on my way home from the dentist," Ms. Ren said, displaying a smile lopsided by **novocaine** as she half-walked, half-pedaled her way down the block.

13   "If they close more streets, I'll have to start finding new routes," she said, again checking, then pedaling on.

14   Store owners whose business has fallen off were less philosophical about the ban.

15   "I think it's a waste of police manpower," said Lin Yinai, manager of a small cluttered advertising design shop. "I've had no new clients all week. This is a city of bicycles. Customers won't come to a place they can't ride to."

16   Others **opined** that Xisidong Avenue was chosen as a testing ground because it is a route favored by officials and the police, who were often stuck for half an hour on the 1,000-foot-long street. Now, the flow of traffic is much improved.

17   Though a number of cyclists were unhappy with the ban, their discomfort certainly came more from the heart than the brain, since there are parallel roads on either side of Xisidong Avenue that still permit **arcane** self-propelled vehicles to pass.

18   Perhaps they are mourning not the closing of a favorite route home, but rather the end of an era.

19   "It's really not too bad, you can always take another route," said A. Fanti, 20, manager of a nearby Muslim restaurant. He said that until the ban he rode his sturdy black bike along Xisidong Avenue every day.

20   "But," he said, "cars are the future."

◆After You Read

Comprehension

1. How are bicyclists being treated in Beijing today?

2. How is this reflected by the change in policy of Xisidong Avenue?

3. How are the bicyclists reacting to the new policy?

4. What is the reaction of store owners?

5. In what way is the new "no bike zone" of Xisidong Avenue an "end of an era"?

6. Do you agree with the bicyclists or the government in this case? Why?

Vocabulary Building

Use each of the words, taken from the reading, in a sentence that shows you understand their meaning.

a.k.a.	novocaine
gridlock	hapless
fanfare	nondescript
arcane	mar
corral (verb)	opine

1. _____

2. _____

3. _____

4. _____

5. _____

6. _____

7. _____

8. _____

9. _____

10. _____

Getting Ready to Read

The next reading is a radio report about bicyclists in another city, San Francisco. This report was presented on National Public Radio's *Morning Edition*. Before you read, discuss these questions with your classmates:

- Are there a lot of bicyclists in your city?

- Are there special paths or services for bicyclists?

- Do you bicycle? Why or why not?

Vocabulary Check

Which of these words do you already know? Check them. Work with a partner to find the meanings of new words. Use a dictionary, if necessary. You can add any new words you learn to your Vocabulary Log.

_____ allegedly   _____ dumpster   _____ strewn

_____ amorphous   _____ monopolize   _____ weld

_____ components   _____ prod

Read

Reading 2: Let Them Ride Bikes

1 *Morning Edition (NPR)*—BOB EDWARDS, HOST: Every month in San Francisco, an organized group of cyclists who call themselves Critical Mass takes to the streets and brings traffic to a halt. Last week, some members left a gift at city hall as part of their campaign to have free bikes available to city residents.

2 From member station KQED in San Francisco, Jason Beaubien reports.

3 JASON BEAUBIEN, KQED REPORTER: Critical Mass has produced traffic headaches for San Francisco, but it's also spurred debate about bicycle commuting. And the **allegedly** leaderless monthly protest ride has become something of an **amorphous** political force in the city.

4 A group of Critical Mass riders pulled up in front of city hall recently and left 10 spraypainted yellow bikes on the steps. John Winston helped organize the event.

5 JOHN WINSTON, ORGANIZER OF CRITICAL MASS FREE BICYCLE DISTRIBUTION: There are free bikes on the streets of San Francisco now. So, if you walk out of your office and you need to go to the copy shop or someplace, if there's a bike sitting there, you can get there a little faster.

6 BEAUBIEN: Winston and other Critical Mass riders donated nine aging 10-speeds and a beat-up Huffy mountain bike in hopes of **prodding** city officials to create a fleet of free bicycles. The idea is currently before the local board of supervisors.

7 It's expected that the free bikes would be old machines that have been painted bright yellow to discourage theft. Several people noted that the spraypainted bicycles left at city hall also have the advantage of being unattractive. One city supervisor even used the word "ugly" to describe the mismatched collection of bikes. But John Winston disagreed.

8 WINSTON: We didn't expect to make them beautiful. We just were going to spraypaint them yellow. And it was a functional thing. We wanted to spraypaint all the **components** so they wouldn't be stolen off the bikes and, you know, the handlebars and the brakes and everything.

9 But, it's actually a really beautiful bike. It says "public bike" on it. It's got a really nice sign that a friend of ours in a sign shop made. It says "for your riding pleasure." There's a little sticker on it that has directions for use. It explains, you know, to ride safely, obey the traffic laws, and, of course, ride at your own risk because this is America.

10 BEAUBIEN: Winston hopes that other people will take out 10-speeds from their basements, put air in the tires, spraypaint them yellow, and leave them out on the sidewalk.

11 Supervisor Gavin Newsom has a more organized plan to make free bicycles available in San Francisco. Newsom introduced legislation recently to place as many as a thousand bikes on the streets. He says the city would probably take some steps to try to keep the bikes from being stolen.

12 GAVIN NEWSOM, SAN FRANCISCO CITY SUPERVISOR: We'll be dealing with **welding** all

the parts so parts cannot be taken. And we'll be incorporating similar to supermarkets, where they have their carts, some deposit idea, where we can actually click the bikes into a sort of a— it's hard to say—a racking system.

13   UNIDENTIFIED WOMAN: A rack thing, yeah.

14   NEWSOM: Or it's probably a dollar, what we're looking at, a dollar deposit. So, people will be encouraged to pick up bikes that are left and **strewn** around the city and bring them back to receive that dollar deposit.

15   BEAUBIEN: Across the country, several cities, including Madison, Wisconsin, Portland, Oregon, Boulder, Colorado, and Austin, Texas, have free bicycle programs.

16   Jan Ward, the downtown transportation co-ordinator in Boulder, says her city has 120 free green bikes available. Ward says the only criticism

of the Boulder program has been that the bikes are used disproportionately by homeless people.

17   JAN WARD, DOWNTOWN TRANSPORTA-TION COORDINATOR, BOULDER, COLORADO: And they tend to adopt them as their own or **monopolize** these bikes.

18   And we're not really too worried about that. They use them all the time. As long as they're not throwing them in the Boulder Creek or trashing them and throwing them in the **dumpster,** we don't really care. As long as they're using them to get around town.

19   BEAUBIEN: Organizers of free bike pro-grams elsewhere say they're not concerned that some of their two-wheelers disappear. All of the bikes are donated, and if they aren't out on the street, it's likely they'd simply be gathering dust in someone's basement.

After You Read

Comprehension

> There are 500,000 bicycles in Amsterdam, which has a population of 800,000.

1. What is "Critical Mass"? What activity do they participate in?

2. What is the new program currently being considered by the local board of supervisors in San Francisco?

3. What plans are there to prevent the bicycles from being stolen?

4. What other cities have similar programs?

5. What criticism is there of the Boulder bike program?

6. Why isn't the Boulder Transportation Coordinator concerned about this problem?

7. What is your opinion of these bike programs?

Test-Taking Tip

Learn how to approach take-home tests:

- Review your notes in advance to re-familiarize yourself with the material.

- Estimate the length of time it will take to finish—allow yourself *at least* that much time, preferably more.

- After you receive your test, assemble everything you will need to complete it.

- Find a place without distractions to work on the test.

- If you are allowed to work with a group, arrange a time you can all meet, or talk over the phone.

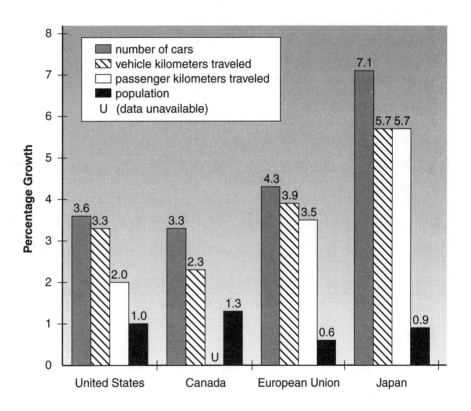

Reading Focus: Practicing Graph Reading

As you learned in Chapter 2, reading graphs accurately is an important skill. Above is a graph concerning private car use in some of the countries of the world. Look at the graph and answer the questions that follow.

1. Which country or area has the highest annual growth rate in number of cars?

2. Which country or area has the lowest annual growth rate in number of cars?

3. Which country or area has the highest annual growth rate in the number of kilometers traveled by car?

4. Which two countries have the highest annual population growth?

5. From highest to lowest, what is the order of the countries' passenger kilometers traveled?

◆ Getting Ready to Read

> Japanese cars are the most popular type of imported car in the U.S.

The next reading concerns a different type of car—a microcar. Before reading, discuss these questions with your class:

- What kind of car do you prefer? Why?
- What qualities are important to you in a car?
- What kind of modern car innovations have you heard about?
- What is a "microcar"?

Vocabulary Check

Which of these words do you already know? Check them. Work with a partner to find the meanings of new words. Use a dictionary, if necessary. Add any new words you learn to your Vocabulary Log.

_____ darting	_____ durable	_____ upholster
_____ dashboard	_____ hassle	_____ yuppie
_____ diesel fuel	_____ savvy	

◆ Read

Reading 3: Microcars Get Big

by Edward M. Gomez

1 Small cars are nothing new. But how about one so tiny you can park it headfirst against, not parallel to, the curb? Just imagine: a car that is so simple a 14-year-old may drive it without a permit, that requires no license plates because it need not be registered, that can be insured at less than a quarter of the rate for regular automobiles, and that is so **durable** and efficient it can travel 100 kilometers on two to three liters of **diesel fuel**.

2 Voilá, the microcar. For about a decade, this urban motorist's dream has been available to thousands of car owners in rural France. In the late 1970s, a handful of automakers developed tiny *voitures sans permis* (or VSPs, "no-license cars") to meet the needs of older consumers in a countryside poorly served by public transportation. Now as metropolitan streets clog with traffic, **savvy** businessmen, fashion models, and young professionals have seized upon the VSP as a practical, low-**hassle** alternative to conventional cars for **darting** around major cities.

3 In a sure sign of trendiness, the miniautos are turning up in advertisements for such **yuppie**-targeting institutions as the Banque Nationale de Paris. About half a dozen firms in the Paris region rent the vehicles for roughly

$75 to $85 a day, including unlimited kilometrage. Weighing in at no more than 350 kilograms and usually measuring 1.4 meters wide by 2.5 meters in length, a VSP can carry two passengers and reach a speed of 45 kilometers an hour. Like motorbikes, VSPs are barred from highways and expressway bypasses. "On paper, VSP specs[1] are those of a motorbike," says Christian Malet, whose Liberty Car service in Paris rents out Marden's tiny Alize model. "But on the road, make no mistake about it, it's a car."

4   Well, sort of. The VSP is a cozy, even comfortable box on wheels with few frills but normal options like a radio and rear windshield wipers. Generally made of sturdy polyester, the body is reinforced by a steel tube frame. The **upholstered** interior typically features durable, molded plastic elements, including a **dashboard** with speedometer, fuel gauge and controls. Seats are adjustable, and heating is standard. The one- to five-horsepower engines made in Italy or Japan have only one forward gear and one for reverse. "The technology is pretty simple," says Patrick Escalier, Paris region director for Marden, "but what more do you need for city driving?"

5   With anxiety over gas prices, the future for the little vehicles may be more attractive than ever. A dozen French VSP manufacturers expect to sell as many as 15,000 units a year.

Martial Howa of Aixam Automobiles, a manufacturer in Aix-les-Bains, estimates that the market will grow 40% in the next two years. "Soon it will not be mostly a French phenomenon," he says. "Already we're exporting 15% of the 5,000 units we produce each year to Germany, Belgium, Switzerland, and Greece." Like Aixam, Société Jeanneau, maker of the Microcar, sells its vehicles to Switzerland without engines: Swiss law requires the installation of electric motors in such vehicles, even though their design is still primitive.

6   VSP users admit that because of their noisy diesel engines, the tiny cars can be painful on the ears. Quieter electric engines would solve that problem, but so far no practical, inexpensive electric power supply has been invented. To reduce exhaust pollution and lessen oil dependency, the French government has set up a committee to encourage development of electric cars.

7   Another VSP disadvantage is the price tag. A typical microcar starts at around $10,500 without options. Still, Paris businessman François-Regis Correard, who owns three VSPs, says they're worth every franc: "Getting around is easy, maintenance is cheap, and you don't get parking tickets." So go ahead. Kick the tires. Take a test ride. They may be tiny, but with word spreading about their features, no wonder microcars are getting so big.

◆ After You Read

Comprehension

1. What is a VSP?

2. Why are they growing more popular?

3. What are their advantages?

4. What are their disadvantages?

5. Why do the Swiss import them without engines?

6. Why don't the French cars have electric engines?

[1]Specs is short for "specifications," meaning the plans or design of something.

se mapping to help you review a text and understand it better. Mapping is a technique in which you show an organization chart of a reading in order to understand its main ideas. For example, a map of the previous reading about free bicycles might look like this:

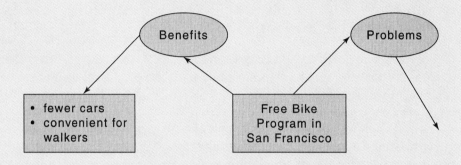

Apply the Strategy

Review the reading about microcars. Then, create a map of the ideas. The word "microcars" has been put in the center box for you.

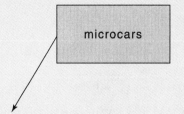

Vocabulary Building

Show that you understand the meanings of the boldface words by completing the sentences.

1. It is important that _____ be **durable** because

   _____.

2. _____ is a **savvy** _____.

3. _____ is really a **hassle**.

4. A **yuppie** is _____.

5. I need to **upholster** _____.

6. You can find _____, _____, and

   _____, on the **dashboard**.

7. _____ was **darting** from place to place because

   _____.

◆ **Getting Ready to Read**
The last reading of this chapter deals with transportation of the future. What do you think the vehicles of tomorrow will look like? Discuss this question with your class.

Vocabulary Check

The following words are found in the reading. Check the ones you already know. For those you do not know, *do not look them up yet.* Complete the reading and locate the unknown words. You will do an additional exercise with these words in the "Vocabulary Building" section.

_____ brainchild   _____ retract

_____ bumper   _____ spoiler

_____ capsule   _____ stabilizer

_____ inclement   _____ trophy

_____ nurture

Use pictures to help you understand descriptions you read. When you encounter a description in a reading, it may help to try to draw what's being described. Many people get a clearer idea if they see what is being described. If you find a description of something in a reading, and it does not include a photograph or picture, you can draw it in order to understand better. You do not need to be artistic to do this—just try to work out on paper the descriptions you read.

Apply the Strategy

The following reading contains descriptions of some new transportation inventions. In the blank spaces near the reading, create diagrams of the invention being described.

◇ Read   Reading 4: Vehicles of the Future

1 *Business Wire*—Award-winning inventor Fred Ferino will be exhibiting his inventions at the Eleventh Annual Invention Convention, held at the Pasadena Convention Center. His inventions have won more than 30 awards and **trophies.**

2   Among them will be the Cafly, an experimental car of the future, designed with a wraparound **bumper** in an egg-like shape that will allow it to bounce off obstacles in a crash. It has wings on top of the car that act as a **spoiler** and **stabilizer.**

3   Exert, an electric- and gas-powered motorcycle, travels at freeway speeds and then from 1 to 20 miles in the electric mode. It can be driven right off the streets into buildings and shopping centers. The windshield is designed to enclose the driver in **inclement** weather and can be **retracted,** if desired.

4   Topco, the airplane of the future, will be displayed in model form. It is double the size of the Boeing 747 and will seat approximately

1,200 people. It replaces regular airplane seats with capsules that provide privacy and built-in conveniences, such as TV, computers, and re-freshments. The **capsules** are shaped so that, in case of a crash, they can float down to earth slowed by a small cone-shaped parachute.

5   Ferino will be showing other inventions, including a car powered by energy. It is totally pollution- and noise-free and costs almost nothing to operate. All of his inventions have safety features. "I want to make the world a better place to live," he said. "There will always be a need for inventions that make the world safer, less expensive, and more pleasant."

6   Many other inventions, both large and small, were shown at the Invention Conven-tion. Inventors from all over the world showed their new inventions and products. The Inven-tion Convention is the **brainchild** of Stephen Paul Gnass, who saw a need to highlight the vital role played by inventors in our society. He said: "The Invention Convention exists to educate and **nurture** the creative person so that he can bring his product to market. The inventor is the hero of the future."

After You Read

Comprehension

1. Who is Fred Ferino?

2. Describe the Cafly.

3. How is the Exert different from typical motorcycles?

4. What is your opinion of the Topco capsule seat?

5. Why did Mr. Gnass start the Invention Convention?

6. Do you agree that "the inventor is the hero of the future"? Why or why not?

Vocabulary Building

You can use context to decode unfamiliar terms, helping you save time in your reading and improving your comprehension. Often, a reading can present a lot of terminology or unfamiliar words. This can make the reading seem especially difficult or time-consuming, especially when you are constantly looking up words in the dictio-nary. However, often a reading gives you the context you need to un-derstand the words without looking them up.

Look at the list of words in the "Vocabulary Check" before the previous reading. Find them in the reading, and look closely at the context. Try to guess what these words mean from the context. After you have done this, you can compare your answers with those of a classmate.

Definitions from context:

1. brainchild _____

   _____

2. bumper _____

   _____

3. capsule _____

   _____

4. inclement _____

   _____

5. nurture _____

   _____

6. retract _____

   _____

7. spoiler _____

   _____

8. stabilizer _____

   _____

9. trophy _____

   _____

PUTTING IT ALL TOGETHER

Read More

Find an article in a newspaper, magazine, or on the Internet that talks about an interesting topic in transportation. Read the article, then write about it in your reading journal. Discuss some of these ideas:

- Ideas in the article that interested you
- Parts that you disagree with
- Parts that confused you
- How this story relates to your life, or to someone you know

Then, report to your class about the article you found.

Discuss

1. Are private cars necessary? Why or why not?

2. What is the best form of daily transportation, in your opinion? Why?

3. Many cities in the world (Salzburg, Austria and Portland, Oregon are two examples) have eliminated cars from their downtown pedestrian areas. Others are considering it. Do you think this is a good idea? Why or why not?

4. What is the biggest transportation problem in the city or town where you live?

Write

1. Think of a transportation invention. Write a description of your invention, and include a drawing. How will your invention solve a current transportation problem?

2. Imagine the world before there were motorized vehicles. Write a short description of daily life without automobiles, buses, airplanes, etc.

3. Consider the transportation problem you discussed in question 4 of the previous section. Write a letter to a city or town official in which you describe the transportation problem as you see it, and propose a solution.

A Survey

In this chapter, you have read and thought about different forms of transportation. But what do other people think? For this final activity, you will design a questionnaire to elicit people's opinions about transportation problems and solutions.

With a group of classmates, design a questionnaire that you will give to at least ten people. The questions you ask should focus on some aspect of transportation that interests you. They can be yes/no questions, multiple choice, or more open-ended ones. Here is a sample of what your questionnaire might look like.

Questionnaire   Respondent # _____

Question 1. _____

Response: ☐ Yes   ☐ No   ☐ Not sure

Question 2. _____

Response: ☐ Yes   ☐ No   ☐ Not sure

(Ask at least 10 questions in your survey.)

After you have gathered your responses, compile them and create a graph or poster explaining the results, as well as a short report to present to your class.

CHECK YOUR PROGRESS

On a scale of 1 to 5, rate how well you have mastered the goals set at the beginning of the chapter:

1 2 3 4 5   find ways to overcome procrastination.

1 2 3 4 5   use mapping to help you review a text.

1 2 3 4 5   use context to decode unfamiliar terms.

1 2 3 4 5   use pictures to help you to understand descriptions you read.

1 2 3 4 5   learn how to do well on take-home tests.

1 2 3 4 5   (your own goal) _____

1 2 3 4 5   (your own goal) _____

If you've given yourself a 3 or lower on any of these goals:

- visit the *Tapestry* web site for additional practice.
- ask your instructor for extra help.
- review the sections of the chapter that you found difficult.
- work with a partner or study group to further your progress.

L ook at the photo. Then discuss these questions with your
classmates:

- What is happening in this photo?
- Do you watch the news regularly? Which news?
- Do you read newspapers often?

10

THAT'S INFOTAINMENT: MEDIA

J ust as access to the world is increasing through travel, technology is improving our ways of communicating over long distances. Telecommunications, computers, and satellites all contribute to our ability to talk to nearly anyone, anywhere, anytime we wish.

The media is an important factor in this growing communications network. The news is no longer merely local, or national, but global. From our living rooms, we can watch the natural disasters and wars happening in other places.

Setting Goals

In this chapter you will learn how to:

◈ accept your mistakes as part of the learning process.

◈ listen effectively to help your reading.

◈ reflect on what you have learned to see your progress.

◈ celebrate your success on tests to keep your motivation high.

What other goals do you have for this chapter? Write two more in the blanks.

_____

_____

Getting Started

This chapter looks at the influence of the media on the world and on individuals. Read these titles:

- "Everything You Could Want Is Out There," an article by Richard Belfield
- "How Media Literacy Can Change the World," an essay by Don Adams and Arlene Goldbard
- "TV Timeout," a newspaper article by Jean Nash Johnson
- "Internet Overtaking TV Among Consumers," a report by Michael Shields

1. Considering the chapter titles, predict the ideas that this chapter will cover. List them here.

   _____

   _____

2. Is Internet use popular among your friends?

   _____

   _____

3. How does television influence our lives, in your opinion?

   _____

   _____

4. Which media do you prefer to get your news from? Explain your answer.

   _____

   _____

5. Look ahead at the pictures and charts in this chapter. What do these tell you about the topic of the chapter?

   _____

   _____

6. What do you want to learn from this chapter? Write down two questions you have about the media.

   _____

   _____

ACADEMIC POWER STRATEGY

Apply the Strategy

Accept your mistakes as part of the learning process. "Nobody's perfect" is a common statement, but what does it really mean? We all make mistakes, and unfortunately, most of us fear mistakes and failure. However, it is important to understand that mistakes offer the potential for growth and learning when you take advantage of them.

The next time you make a mistake—for example, complete an assignment incorrectly, use the wrong word in your essay, sign up for a class that isn't what you want, or read the wrong assignment—take the following steps in order to learn from your error.

1. Notice the mistake. Write in your journal what the mistake was. You need to notice your mistakes in order to correct them. Don't hide what you did; it's easier to fix errors than cover them up. And don't blame someone else. It was *you* who chose the wrong word, not the dictionary writer; *you* read the wrong assignment, not the teacher who gave you the assignment.

2. Write what you learned from the mistake. How will you avoid doing the same thing next time?

3. Act on your mistake. Take a positive step that shows you learned from it. If you forgot an assignment that was due, buy yourself a new appointment book and note all your assignments.

4. Celebrate learning from your mistake. Mistakes show that you are taking risks, and have a goal in mind. When you notice your mistake and take action, congratulate yourself for really learning!

LANGUAGE LEARNING STRATEGY

Learn to listen effectively in order to help your reading. When you use different methods of gathering information, all of your skills improve. So, listening can help reading, reading can help

(continued on next page)

listening, speaking can help thinking, and so forth. How? By increasing your awareness of vocabulary, themes, topics, and other issues, listening can be used to help make you a more aware reader.

Apply the Strategy

Watch a national news show on CNN or any other television network, then answer these questions. On your own, use the following spaces to take notes as you watch the news broadcast.

1. Name of television network I watched: _____

2. Describe the major international news story of the day.

   _____

   _____

3. Was there any film shown as part of the story? If so, describe it.

   _____

   _____

4. Describe one other international news story that was reported on the program.

   _____

   _____

   _____

◈ Getting Ready to Read

How does international media affect the world? Discuss this question with your class. Different types of governments and populations have different concerns about the availability of information. The next article looks at how governments and people might control, and be controlled by, the spread of information.

Vocabulary Check

Which of these words do you already know? Check them. Work with a partner to find the meanings of new words. Use a dictionary, if necessary. Add any new words you learn to your Vocabulary Log.

_____ anarchist	_____ cyberspace	_____ exponential
_____ cornucopia	_____ ethos	_____ hypertext

_____ lateral	_____ niche	_____ staggeringly
_____ leaflet	_____ prevail	_____ totalitarian
_____ libel	_____ regime	_____ upside
_____ ludicrous	_____ slothful	

 Read

Reading 1: Everything You Could Want Is Out There

by Richard Belfield

1   A friend was recently selling software in China. He demonstrated the Internet to some government officials. They were very impressed until the interpreter said rather anxiously, "Your hosts would like to know how they can control it."

2   "Ah," said the salesman, "they can't." And that's the rub.[1] The Internet is not controlled by any government or multinational—and what is more, it is hard to see how it ever could be. Although governments can control and manipulate what is in the papers and on television, the net is just too big and too global for anyone to get a grip on it.

3   It continues to grow **exponentially,** with few countries left untouched. Every **totalitarian regime** knows that to advance they must plug into the global telephone system. But as soon as they do, they risk losing control of the flow of information.

4   Modems are now **staggeringly** cheap, and it's possible to dial in from just about anywhere in the world. This makes the Internet—potentially—a great democratizer. The global media giant Ted Turner has long argued that satellite TV stations such as CNN (http://www.cnn.com) are a tremendous force for democratic change. Pirate feeds[2] of CNN and other channels into East Germany fueled the liberation movement, helping to create the tide of change that swept away the Berlin Wall.

5   For CNN, now read the Internet. The difference is that the net is interactive, allowing users to seek and share the information they want, and it's therefore significantly more powerful.

6   At this point in the argument, the Internet's critics usually raise the issue of pornography as the unacceptable downside of a lack of control. The European Union is currently planning to spend $8 million to devise guidelines to protect net users from sites that are "offensive to human dignity."

7   It's wasted money. Porn will always be there on the net, though the problem is easily overstated. It is harder to find porn on the net than in the average newsagent's and, anyway, for anxious parents, there is software that can limit their children's access to it.

8   What the censors find hard to grasp is that the net does not recognize national boundaries, so what applies in the most liberal countries applies everywhere. The American judges who threw out the Communications Decency Act (see http://www.aclu.org), Bill Clinton's clumsy attempt to restrict the net, argued that they could not legislate on matters of taste for different communities. In their view, what would be perfectly acceptable

[1]That's the problem.

[2]A pirate feed is an illegal transmission of a television or radio broadcast.

in New York could be deeply offensive to god-fearing Christians in middle America. They did not conclude that the Christians therefore had the right to restrict everyone else's freedom. Instead, they argued that the web is "a never-ending global conversation" which had to be protected from governments, not controlled by them.

9   This global conversation is producing new communities of interest, sharing new forms of information exchange. The net is defining itself by the huge growth in user groups, people around the world who have never met but who share a common interest, whether it is in Greek architecture or the CIA. For them, the net is an open meeting place, where all are equal and the **prevailing ethos** is sharing rather than owning.

10   This constant flow of uncontrolled information makes the web a great equalizer. If you search for "McDonald's" you will get many opposition sites long before you reach the golden arches. King of these is the McLibel site (http://www.mcspotlight.org), spawned out of the **ludicrous libel** action brought by the company against two penniless **anarchists** for distributing a **leaflet** that few people had read. The site is now the focus for opposition to McDonald's (and other multinationals) worldwide.

11   This explosion of new media—particularly user groups and **niche** providers—has shaken up the traditional news producers. Many have fought back with strong brand-name web sites. The *Times* (http://www.the-times.co.uk) has 1.2 million users, the *Telegraph* (http://www.telegraph.co.uk) just under a million. For news junkies everywhere, the BBC site (http://www.bbc.co.uk) is a must.

12   But the balance of power is shifting towards the consumer. Newspapers survived the arrival of television because they are foldable, transportable, and convenient. In the digital age, news provision is changing again. Net households get their up-to-date news when they want it, from where they want it and in the form they want it—rather than at a set time every day. The model is that of a 24-hour newspaper, printed moments before purchase, as opposed to that of television, with its three main bulletins a day.

13   As well as changing our media behavior, the Internet is provoking new ways of thinking. Previous generations of schoolchildren learnt in a linear, two-dimensional form, one fact following another. Knowledge is now stored and accessed three-dimensionally through the use of **hypertext** links, which connect the same word on different pages. As a result, the digital generation thinks more **laterally** and in a freer form than their parents. The **upside** for self-motivating kids is that there is a **cornucopia** of knowledge available. The downside is that the intellectually **slothful** will suffer—but then they always did.

14   For adults, the net is generating new forms of commerce. In the past year, the net has become a huge electronic souk[3] in which virtually anything can be located and bought. Thirty years after Marshall McLuhan,[4] it is not so much a global village as a global marketplace.

15   Above all, the net is incomprehensibly vast. I am always baffled by people who say they cannot find anything interesting here. It's like walking into the British Library and saying there aren't any interesting books. Think of it as the world's museums and libraries rolled into one.

16   Then imagine what it would be like to find anything you wanted and be constantly seduced by new and exciting stuff wherever you went. That's **cyberspace** for you. And the best thing of all is that people everywhere are doing it for themselves—as producers, not just consumers.

---

[3]Souk is the Arabic word for marketplace.

[4]Marshall McLuhan is considered to be a pioneer theorist in explaining the media and its influence on consumers.

◆ After You Read

Comprehension

According to Nielsen Media Research, 58% of Internet users are male; 42% are female; and 48.7% have college degrees.

1. Why can't the Internet be controlled, according to the article?

2. What problem do totalitarian governments face in trying to advance their societies in the age of the Internet?

3. How may the Internet become a "democratizer"? Why do you think the author qualifies this statement with the word "potentially"?

4. Why does the author think that the Internet is more powerful than global television media?

5. Why does the author think that trying to ban pornography on the Internet is "wasted money"? Do you agree?

6. What was the Communications Decency Act? Why was it defeated?

7. How has news provision changed in the past? How is it changing currently?

8. How is the Internet provoking new ways of thinking, according to the author?

9. How is the Internet benefiting people, according to the author?

10. What does the author mean when he says, "And the best thing of all is that people everywhere are doing it for themselves—as producers, not just consumers"?

Test-Taking Tip

Celebrate your success on tests to keep your motivation high and give yourself encouragement for future tests.

• Treat yourself to a special meal or favorite food.

• Get together with friends for a relaxing evening.

• Buy yourself a new poster for your wall, or frame your favorite photograph.

• _____ (list your own reward)

Vocabulary Building

Choose the correct words to go into the blanks in the sentences. Each word is used only once.

anarchist	niche
cornucopia	prevail
exponential	regime
hypertext	staggering
lateral	totalitarian
manipulate	upside

1. If you manage something cleverly, you ＿＿＿＿＿＿＿ it.

2. Another word for "sideways" is ＿＿＿＿＿＿＿.

3. A(n) ＿＿＿＿＿＿＿ doesn't believe in government control.

4. If something grows extremely rapidly, it's often called ＿＿＿＿＿＿＿ growth.

5. A ＿＿＿＿＿＿＿ is another way of saying political system.

6. The linking of words on the Internet or in software is also called ＿＿＿＿＿＿＿.

7. A wide assortment of things is also called a(n) ＿＿＿＿＿＿＿.

8. If a country has an enormous debt, it is often called a ＿＿＿＿＿＿＿ sum of money.

9. If you find your ＿＿＿＿＿＿＿, you have found your role or function in life.

10. If you triumph over hardships, you are said to ＿＿＿＿＿＿＿.

11. The positive aspect of something is its ＿＿＿＿＿＿＿.

12. A government that attempts to have complete control of its people is called a ＿＿＿＿＿＿＿ government.

◁ Getting Ready to Read

The next reading argues for something called "media literacy," or an understanding of how television stories and programming can manipulate viewers. What does media literacy mean to you? Watch the CNN video, then discuss this question with your class.

TUNING IN: "Multi-Media Education"

Watch the CNN video about multi-media education. Then, discuss these questions with your class:

- What does "multi-media" education refer to?
- What kinds of projects do the students participate in?
- What are the advantages of this classroom?

© CNN

Vocabulary Check

Which of these words and phrases do you already know? Check them. Work with a partner to find the meanings of new words. Use a dictionary, if necessary. Add any new words you learn to your Vocabulary Log.

_____ citizenry	_____ fundamental	_____ proliferation
_____ couch potato	_____ grapple	_____ ratify
_____ dynamic	_____ mainstream	_____ thrall
_____ forum	_____ passivity	_____ undermine
_____ foster	_____ pep squad	

Reading Focus: Strategy Practice

Monitor your reading speed for this passage. (See page 81 for a description of improving reading speed.)

Read

Reading 2: How Media Literacy Can Change the World

by Don Adams & Arlene Goldbard   Starting Time: _____:_____

1 Democracy requires critical thinking. Almost everyone agrees that the ability to read and write should be a **fundamental** human right, extended to everyone. We understand that a person who cannot read is in **thrall** to those who can. You cannot enter the developed world as a full human subject unless you can break and master the code of the word. Today, literacy doesn't stop with words and numbers. To enter social and political debates as a full participant, one must also break the thrall of the magic box and master its secrets. If we fail to adopt media literacy—a basic knowledge of how and why media images are chosen—as an essential goal of public cultural policy, we doom ourselves to be forever in the grip

of the powerful interests who own and control the mass media. The global **proliferation** of electronic mass media has excited deep feeling and passionate debate. Most alarming to observers around the world has been the **passivity** the mass media seem to breed in most people; it displaces and **undermines** social life, community activities, and other creative pursuits. We jokingly call it being **couch potatoes.** As a society, we need to **foster** a more **dynamic** relationship between the **citizenry** and the media, one that does not stop when the program ends and the TV is turned off. For those who aspire to greater democracy in public life, our greatest challenge is transforming the media into a tool for democratic change.

2   Achieving this will require starting from square one. People without some special interest in the field find it hard to **grapple** with the idea that media is a public and political issue. This is not surprising, since one of the things our mass media do best is pound home the inevitability of the way that they are currently organized, ideally suited to their role as the **pep squad** for our consumer society. Their self-**ratifying** quality makes it hard even to imagine that the media can be changed in any way.

3   The massive, interlocking complex of business interests that make up the **mainstream** media have been allowed to develop pretty much as they wish, in the pursuit of commercial success. Meanwhile, the essential public issue—the media role as our primary public **forum,** its tendency to erode democratic life—has been pushed further and further into the background.

4   It is necessary that we think about and promote a public policy that looks at what role media should play in our society and how people can participate in shaping television and other mass media that affect all of our lives. Such a public policy could counter the imbalances that result from the domination of a country's cultural industries by commercial interests. We cannot expect the commercial arena to accommodate the goals that should be the essence of this public policy: nurturing diversity, stimulating and supporting creativity, and encouraging active participation and interaction in community and political life.

Ending Time: _____ : _____
Number of minutes spent reading:

_____ divided by 491 words = _____
words per minute

◆ After You Read

Comprehension

1. What do the authors mean when they say "democracy requires critical thinking"?

2. How do the authors define "media literacy"?

3. Why is media literacy important?

4. Do the authors think that the media can be changed? What part of the reading tells you that?

5. Who has controlled the media, according to the authors?

6. What are the goals of public policy, according to the reading? Do you agree?

◇**Vocabulary Building**

Look at the sentences below. Rephrase each sentence by substituting a synonym for the word or phrase that is underlined. You may have to change some of the rest of the sentence slightly, but don't change the meaning.

1. We understand that a person who cannot read <u>is in thrall</u> to those who can.

   _____

   _____

   _____

2. To enter social and political debates as a full participant one must also break <u>the thrall</u> of <u>the magic box</u> and master its secrets.

   _____

   _____

   _____

3. We need to <u>foster</u> a more <u>dynamic</u> relationship between the <u>citizenry</u> and the media, one that does not stop when the program ends and the TV is turned off.

   _____

   _____

   _____

4. Achieving this will require <u>starting from square one.</u>

   _____

   _____

   _____

5. This is not surprising, since one of the things our mass media do best is <u>pound home</u> the <u>inevitability</u> of the way that they are currently organized, ideally suited to their role as <u>the pep squad</u> for our consumer society.

   _____

   _____

   _____

   _____

◆ **Getting Ready to Read**

The following reading talks about an unusual event: the "TV Turnoff," a time when families are asked to turn off their televisions for an entire week and do other things. Discuss these questions with your class:

- What do you think of this idea?
- Could you go without television for a week?

Vocabulary Check

Which of these words and phrases do you already know? Check them. Work with a partner to find the meanings of new words. You can add any new words you learn to your Vocabulary Log.

_____ armoire	_____ go cold turkey
_____ catch phrase	_____ subliminal
_____ dissension	_____ viewership

> In 1977, 16.6% of American households had cable television. In 1995, 65.3% did.

"What'll it be—entertainment news or entertainment?"

Strategy Practice: Scanning

Review the Scanning Strategy on page 55. Scan the following article for this information. Work as quickly as you can.

1. In what year did "Turnoff Week" begin? _____

2. How many people have participated? _____

3. How many television viewers were lost between May 1996 and April 1997? _____

4. How many minutes of TV does the average child watch a week? _____

5. How many killings will an average elementary-school child see on television? _____

◆Read

Reading 3: TV Timeout

by Jean Nash Young

1 John McMillan grew up on an Iowa farm, no TV.

2   His wife, Erica, who grew up in Texas, watched lots of TV as a child.

3   Together they have developed good viewing habits, and now their mission is to raise their children to be TV savvy.

4   "Today, TV is different from when I watched. There's more violence, more **subliminal** messages and sexuality," Mrs. McMillan says.

5   As the Dallas-area family and many others across the country prepare to **go cold turkey** for National TV-Turnoff Week, "media literacy" is the new **catch phrase** for parents, educators, and experts. All agree children should be taught how to watch TV.

6   Turnoff Week premiered in April 1995, and more than 8 million people across the country have participated through the years, according to promoters. The campaign appears to be having an effect on TV **viewership.**

7   On the heels of the April 1997 campaign, the May sweeps period[1] that immediately followed showed a significant drop in prime-time[2] viewing from 1996—more than 1 million households, according to a recent A.C. Nielsen Company[3] measurement.

8   Still, media and education experts are divided over the campaign's ultimate effect. "TV is a thief of time, and it can rob your little one

---

[1]Sweeps period refers to the time during the year in which the popularity of television shows is measured. The popularity determines the amount that is charged for advertising.

[2]Prime time is the viewing hours between 8 and 11 p.m. on weeknights. It is called "prime time" because it is when the most viewers are watching television.

[3]A.C. Nielson is the company that performs ratings measurements on television programs.

of a childhood, " says Joan Anderson, author of *Getting Unplugged*.

9 But Lauryn Axelrod passionately disagrees: "TV has value. If you ban it entirely from your child's life, it's like throwing out the baby with the bath water," says the media literacy expert and co-author of *TV-Proof Your Kids*.

10 "To turn the TV off for a week and expect that to solve the problem habitually is unrealistic," Ms. Axelrod says. "It is a part of the culture, and we can't escape that."

11 Television is truly an inescapable part of a child's life, she says. The real question is how much is too much?

12 "We simply want people to watch less. We want Americans to reduce dramatically and voluntarily the amount of TV they watch," says Monte Burke, spokesman for TV-Free America, the Washington, D.C., nonprofit organization that sponsors the annual campaign.

13 The group is particularly interested in children, because of the powerful influence of television on growing minds.

14 The average child watches 1,680 minutes of TV a week. By the time that child finishes elementary school, he or she will have seen 8,000 killings on the tube, according to the group.

15 Ms. Axelrod sees in that statistic all the more reason for getting parents involved in what their children are watching. "It's important that children learn early to separate the realities from the fantasies."

16 Generally, says Ms. Axelrod, parents manage their children's television viewing in one of three ways: They ban TV viewing altogether; they allow the kids to watch selectively; or they set no boundaries. "Many studies have shown that the kid most adjusted is the one in the middle, " she says.

17 The McMillans see themselves as among those who are selective about television. "We do watch some TV, and we watch as a family. We stick mostly to videos and educational programs. Disney and the Learning Channel are mainly what we watch," Mrs. McMillan says.

18 Because of their different TV upbringings, the McMillans had to work out what role the medium would play in their lives from the start of their marriage. But that made it easier for them to discuss the role of television in the lives of their children: John, 5, and Justin, 3. "My family didn't watch any TV when I was growing up," Mr. McMillan says. "It wasn't until college that I got to watch a lot of TV, and I did."

19 It is important to get into the habit of doing family activities other than watching television, the McMillans say. "We're always looking for something to do with our free time, and it usually doesn't involve TV," says Mr. McMillan.

20 The McMillans also spend time each day talking with their children or reading books together. And, they keep the kids active outdoors.

21 "I try to have a family dinner every night, even if it's just me and the boys," says Mrs. McMillan, who is pregnant with their third child. Mr. McMillan is vice president of a local construction firm and often works long hours.

22 Ms. Axelrod says the McMillans are a model, and she hopes they continue constructive viewing habits as their children grow older. "All I insist on is parental involvement."

23 While Ms. Axelrod is critical of the Turnoff campaign, she doesn' t believe that people should not participate.

24 "But, you need preparation to survive a week like that," she says. "You tell a kid who has been watching TV steadily they can't watch, you're going to have horrible screaming. You end up with a week of **dissension**."

25 On the other hand, Ms. Anderson, the author of *Getting Unplugged*, says a week without TV can have great benefit.

26 Ms. Anderson, whose latest book addresses TV-watching and computer and video-game habits, also wrote *Breaking the TV Habit,* which helped bring national attention to the subject 10 years ago. She believes TV-Turnoff Week can be a first step toward breaking habits that keep family members apart.

27 "TV-Turnoff Week [at least] involves the whole family. . . . You discover being together is not so bad."

28   Children crave live interaction, "yet, so many parents use the TV as a baby sitter," Ms. Anderson says.

29   "I talk to teachers, and they tell me real sad stories about the kids coming into the classrooms tired from staying up late with TV. . . . Middle-class latchkey kids[4] coming in and wanting and needing to chat with teachers because no one at home will. They are missing that fundamental interaction at home . . . they're not communicating with parents."

30   That is why Ms. Axelrod, the media literacy expert, continues to push the schools for media education. She wants teachers to take on some of the responsibility of educating children about the medium.

31   "Parents who have dialogues with children about TV and who engage them in critical thinking about the programs they watch fare better at offering children perspective. But not many parents do," Ms. Axelrod says.

32   "Children should never have TVs in their bedrooms. Adults should never have a TV in the bedroom. It makes it too easy to go your separate ways in the evenings instead of paying attention to what's important."

33   Make TV watching more formal, Ms. Axelrod suggests. If possible, cut back to one TV set. "If you have [a family member] who is a TV nut, place the TV in an **armoire** that closes and is out of sight, and plan your watching and do a lot of negotiating."

34   It may be unrealistic, as Ms. Axelrod points out, to expect continued strict observance, but experts say all parents should try to tune in to how the family is watching TV.

35   Request that each member of your household pick at least one good habit to hold on to after the campaign, Ms. Anderson says.

36   "Ask your husband to agree to no TV during dinner. Or remove the TV from Johnny's room and insist that he watches TV with the rest of the family."

37   Small steps, true, but they can lead to some long-term good habits.

◆ **After You Read**

Comprehension

1. How is television different now than when Mrs. McMillan was a child?

2. What is "National TV-Turnoff Week"?

3. Why do media experts disagree about the "Turnoff Week's" effects?

4. Why do some experts want children to watch less television?

5. What is wrong with using television as a "babysitter," according to some experts?

6. What are some ways to cut back on television watching, according to the article?

7. What are the three types of "television upbringing"? Which upbringing seems most successful? Which one were you brought up with?

[4]Latchkey kids are children who are left home alone after school until their parents return from work. They are often kept entertained by watching television.

◈ Getting Ready to Read

In 1997, one second of Super Bowl advertising cost as much as a 30-second commercial did during the first Super Bowl in 1967. A 30-second ad in 1997 cost $1.2 million.

The last report in this chapter talks about the Internet's influence on television. Although the previous article talks about a campaign to get people to watch less TV, the following one shows that this might already be happening. This is not because people don't like television—but because it seems they are spending more free time on the Internet instead. Do you think the Internet is a better way to spend time than television? Why or why not? Discuss this with your class.

Vocabulary Check

Which of these words do you already know? Check them. Work with a partner to find the meanings of new words. Use a dictionary, if necessary. Add any new words you learn to your Vocabulary Log.

_____ analog   _____ horde

_____ converge   _____ leverage

_____ digital

◈ Read

Reading 4: Internet Overtaking TV Among Consumers

by Michael Shields

1   The Internet is drawing **hordes** of people away from their television sets but will have to become more like TV if it wants to boost its mass appeal to consumers, computer industry executives say.

2   In any event, the two media are **converging** rapidly in a trend that will accelerate when **digital** broadcasting replaces the dominant **analog** television system around the world, they said at the World Economic Forum's annual meeting in Davos.

3   "We recently completed a survey of our customers, who told us in the consumer segment that they prefer to be on the Internet than to watch television at home," said Michael Dell, the 31-year-old chairman of computer maker Dell Computer Corporation.

4   Raymond Lane, president of Redwood City, California, software company Oracle Corporation, predicted the distinction between television and the Internet—the global network of computer networks—would soon start to blur.

5   "There will be a convergence in the next couple of years, maybe sooner than that," he told a panel discussion.

6   This will lead to customized newspapers and video called up at the touch of a button as a powerful rival to television.

7   "This is a slowly adapting marketplace, but I think broadcast television, as alternatives for profiling and customization are offered, will diminish," Lane said.

8   Computer workstation maker Sun Microsystems, Inc.'s chief technology officer, Eric Schmidt, said the breakthrough will come when digital broadcasting puts television on the same technological footing as computers.

9   "At the point when the television signal that the average person gets is digital, there is tremendous **leverage** to browsing the Internet model and the digital bits that you see on your screen," he said.

10   "What I worry about is that we will hit a limit in our industry in the number of people to whom it makes sense to be online," he added.

11   "To get to the 70, 80, 90 percent kind of market that television has, we are going to have to have a model that looks a lot more like television and a lot more like entertainment than any of us have seen so far."

12   Lane was a bit more skeptical of forecasts that the Internet could crowd out television in the battle for consumers.

13   "The consumer is slow to adapt, always. You can push the cost down and simplify things, but consumer behavior is very, very difficult to change," he said. "This is going to be a very predictable and relatively slow-growth rate for our industry."

14   On the hardware front, Lane said the trend was toward affordable computers rather than high-powered machines.

15   "I am much more optimistic you will start to see very simple, low-cost devices. You don't need the complexity if you just have a limited set of tasks, if you do e-mail all day or are connected to a local area (computer) network," he said.

◆ **After You Read**

Comprehension

1. Why does the author think the Internet needs to be more like TV?

2. What technology will speed up the convergence of the Internet and television, according to the article?

3. What are some of the results of this convergence?

4. Why does Mr. Lane think that the Internet won't crowd television out?

5. At the time the article was written, what was the trend in the computer industry? Is that different from the trends today?

PUTTING IT ALL TOGETHER

Read More

Find an article in a newspaper, magazine, or on the Internet that talks about an interesting topic in media and communication. Read the article, then write in your reading journal about it. Discuss some of these ideas:

- Ideas in the article that interested you

- Parts that you disagreed with

- Parts that confused you

- How this story relates to your life, or to someone you know

Then, report to your class about the article you found.

Discuss

What is censorship? Review the articles in this chapter. Where is there discussion of censorship? Do you think TV should be censored? Should the Internet? Discuss these questions, and any others you might think of concerning censorship, with your class. Make notes of the major points made during the discussion.

With a group of classmates, review your notes from the class discussion. Develop a topic for debate from your discussion.

Divide your group into two equal parts. Half of your group should argue for one side of the issue you chose, and the other side should argue for the other.

You may want to use the following outline to help you develop your arguments.

Topic: _____

State your side's opinion in one sentence:

_____

_____

_____

Reasons you believe this: (Again, state each reason as a sentence).

1. _____

   _____

   _____

2. _____

   _____

   _____

3. _____

   _____

   _____

4. _____

   _____

   _____

(Use an additional piece of paper if you need more space.)

Present your debate to the class. Each side should get the same amount of time to present its arguments.

Write

1. What is your favorite media? Write a short essay explaining what type of media you prefer (print media such as magazines and news-papers, television, radio, Internet, etc.) and why.

2. In your journal, write about a television program that has had an impact on your life.

3. How is American television different from the television produced in your home country? Write a comparison between televi-sion shows in your country and those produced in the U.S.

Project

Create your own news broadcast. With a small group of classmates, find a current newspaper and read the major stories. From these sto-ries, create a television news script; that is, turn each major story into a one- or two-minute broadcast script. What difficulties did you encounter? Practice reading your scripts, and then give your news broadcast for your class.

LANGUAGE LEARNING STRATEGY

Reflect on what you have learned to help you get a feeling of success and to see the progress you have made. You have ac-complished a lot. Whether you have completed the entire book up to this point, or skipped around, you have no doubt improved your reading, learned new facts, considered new ideas, held successful dis-cussions with your classmates, and increased your vocabulary. It's time to congratulate yourself.

Apply the Strategy

Make a list of some skills and strategies you have acquired while working with this book and identify the readings with which you practiced this skill. Use the chart on the following page.

(continued on next page)

Skills/Strategy	Reading With Which I Practiced This Skill or Strategy

CHECK YOUR PROGRESS

On a scale of 1 to 5, rate how well you have mastered the goals set at the beginning of the chapter:

1 2 3 4 5   accept your mistakes as part of the learning process.

1 2 3 4 5   listen effectively to help your reading.

1 2 3 4 5   reflect on what you have learned to see your progress.

1 2 3 4 5   celebrate your success on tests to keep your motivation high.

1 2 3 4 5   (your own goal) _____

1 2 3 4 5   (your own goal) _____

If you've given yourself a 3 or lower on any of these goals:

- visit the *Tapestry* web site for additional practice.
- ask your instructor for extra help.
- review the sections of the chapter that you found difficult.
- work with a partner or study group to further your progress.

APPENDIX 1: USEFUL INTERNET SITES

Following are some internet sites you might find useful in your reading and research. Although it is unlikely that any of these sites would go out of business, remember that the internet is always changing, so you might find a "404" (file not found) in some cases.

The Newbury House Dictionary:
http://nhd.heinle.com

CNN: http://www.cnn.com

The U.S. White House:
http://www.whitehouse.gov

Biography:
http://www.biography.com

Encyclopedia:
http://www.encyclopedia.com

The *New York Times*:
http://www.nytimes.com

E-Library:
http://www.elibrary.com

The Internet Movie Database:
http://www.imdb.com

The *Atlantic Monthly* magazine:
http://www.theatlantic.com

APPENDIX 2:
FILMS RELATED TO THE THEMES OF THIS BOOK

The films listed below relate to the chapter themes. If you can, rent some of these videos to help your understanding of the ideas presented by the readings. The main theme of the video is in parentheses after the title.

**Chapter 1. Thinking Globally:
A Changing World**

Cry, The Beloved Country (South Africa)

Missing (South America)

The Unbearable Lightness of Being
(Czechoslovakia)

The Year of Living Dangerously (Indonesia)

**Chapter 2. On the Move:
Population and Immigration**

El Norte (Central American immigration)

Green Card (U.S. citizenship)

The Joy Luck Club (Asian-Americans)

Chapter 3. All Talk: Language

Talk Radio (talk)

The Battle of Gregorio Cortez (translation)

The Miracle Worker (Helen Keller story)

**Chapter 4. Food for Thought:
Nutrition**

Fatso (overweight)

The Karen Carpenter Story (anorexia)

Babette's Feast (eating well)

Chapter 5. Not Child's Play: Work

Norma Rae (labor unions)

Blue Collar (work)

Chapter 6. Let There Be Peace on Earth: Peace & Conflict

The War Between Us (Canada-Japan)

Gone with the Wind (U.S. Civil War)

Soldier of Orange (World War II; Dutch)

Apocalypse Now (U.S.-Vietnam)

Chapter 7. Saving the Planet: Ecology

Silkwood (nuclear accidents)

Gorillas in the Mist (endangered species)

Fly Away Home (nature)

Never Cry Wolf (wolves)

Chapter 8. Flights of Fancy: Travel

Vacation (car trip)

Before Sunrise (European trip)

The Long, Long Trailer (car travel)

Chapter 9. Going Places: Alternative Transportation

Breaking Away (bicycles)

Easy Rider (motorcycles)

Silver Streak (train)

Trains, Planes, & Automobiles (transportation comedy)

Chapter 10. That's Infotainment: Media

Network (television)

Sneakers (computers)

The Net (Internet)

Up Close and Personal (newspaper)

You've Got Mail (Internet)

SKILLS INDEX

PHOTO CREDITS